LYNNE PICKERING

ART & INTERIORS

BEACH ART

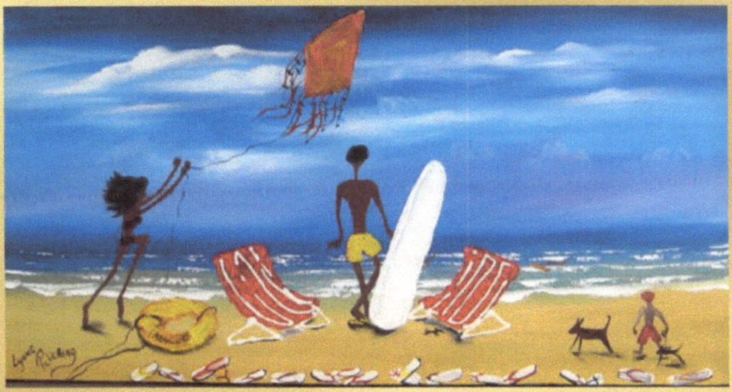

ISBN 13:978-1516952182
ISBN 10: 151 6952189

Book design Lynne Pickering

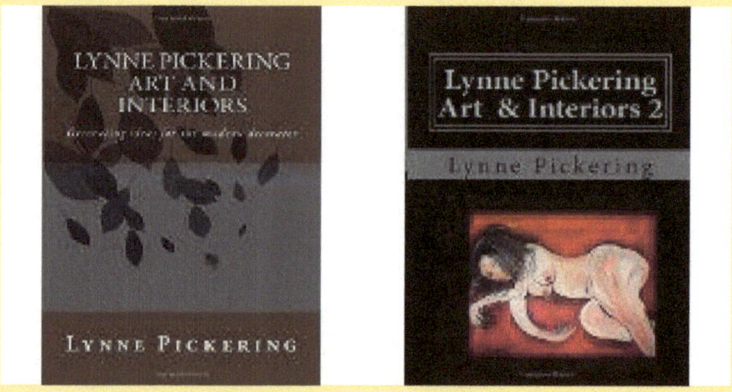

Other art books by Lynne Pickering

TABLE OF CONTENTS

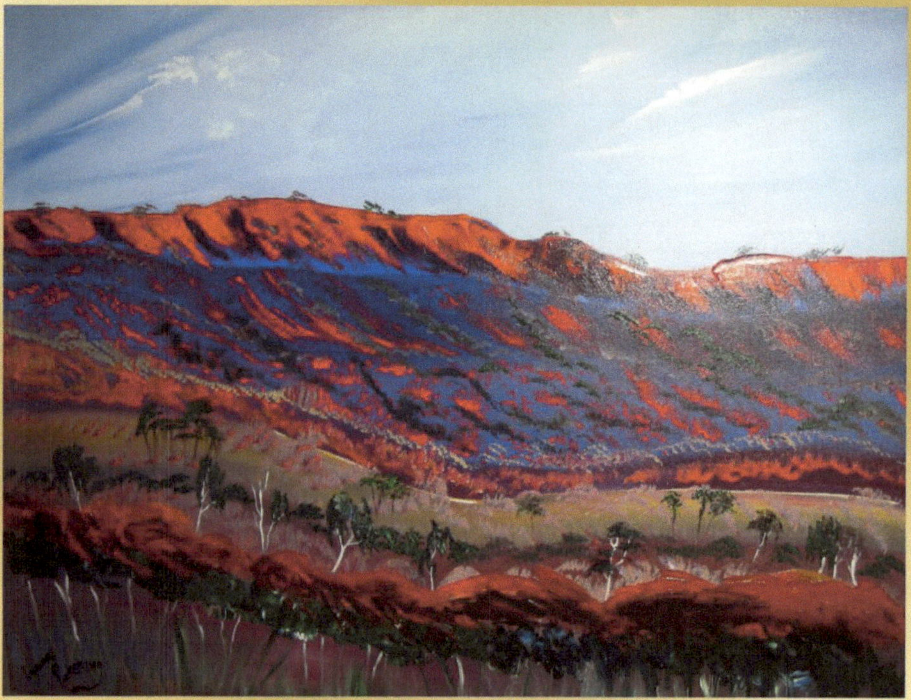

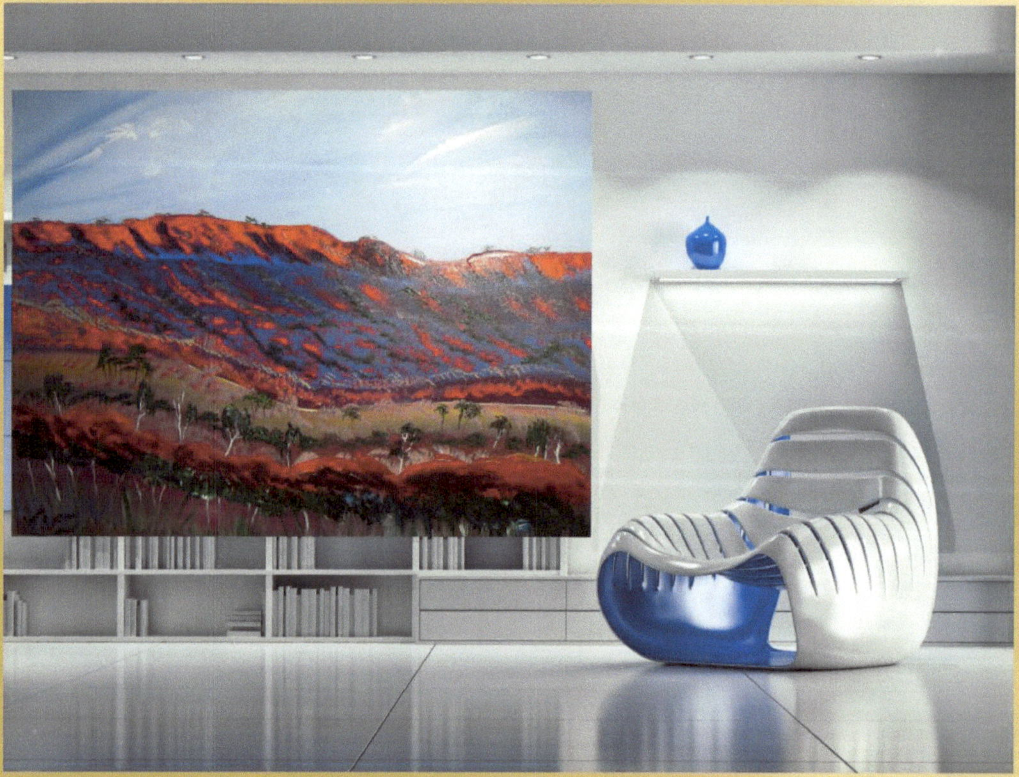

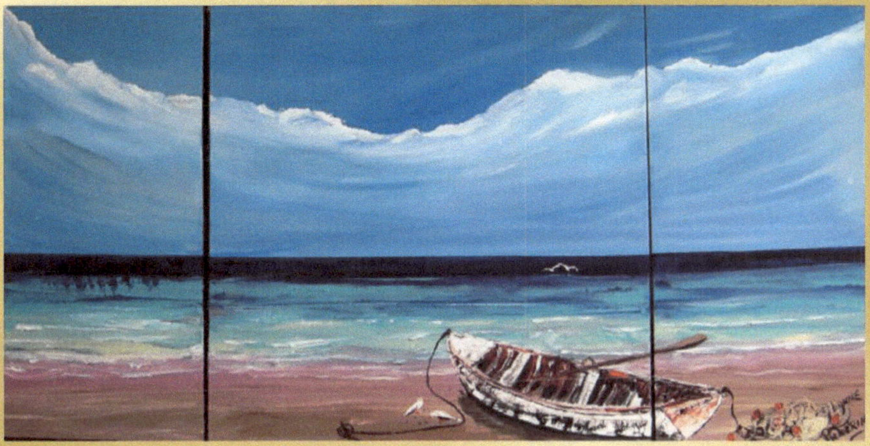

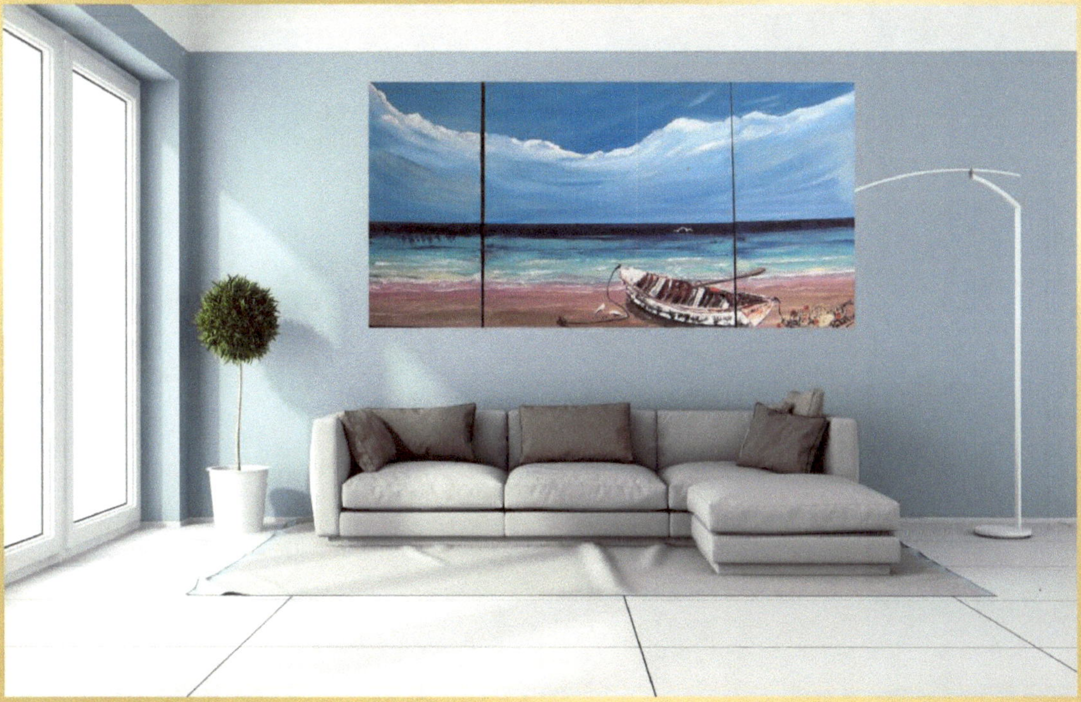

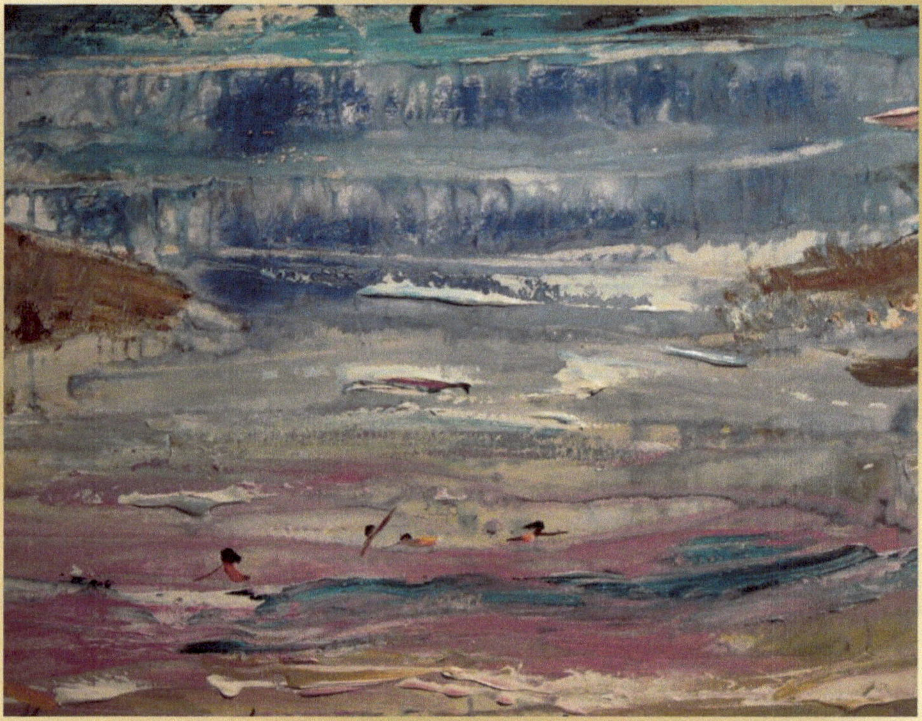

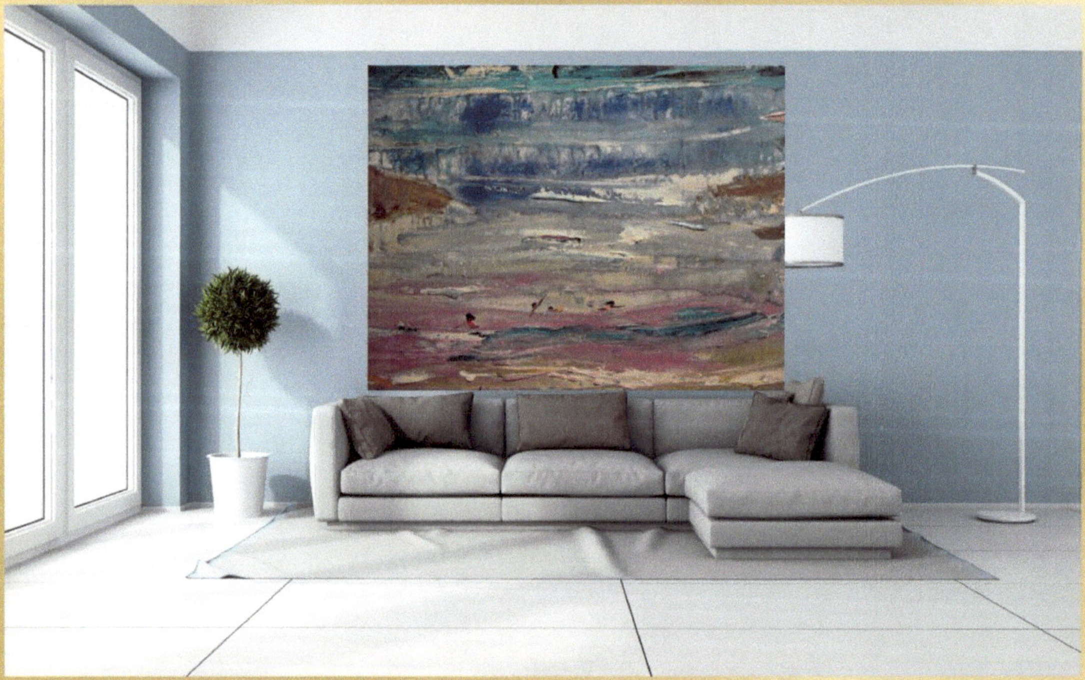

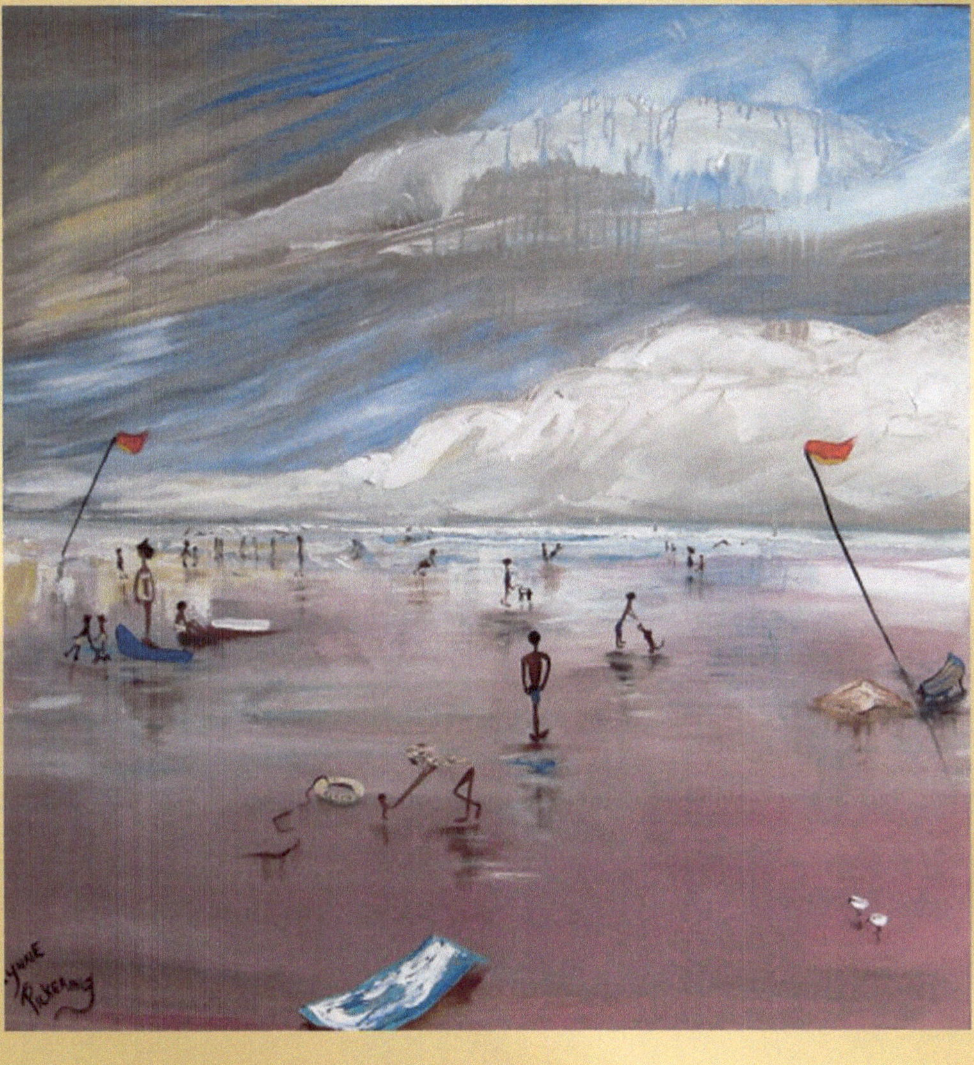

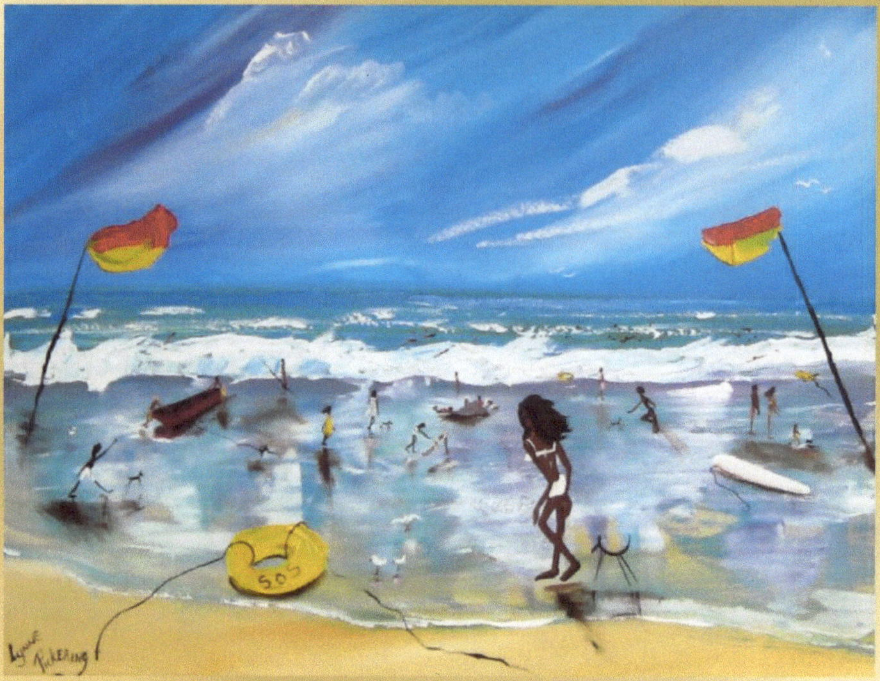

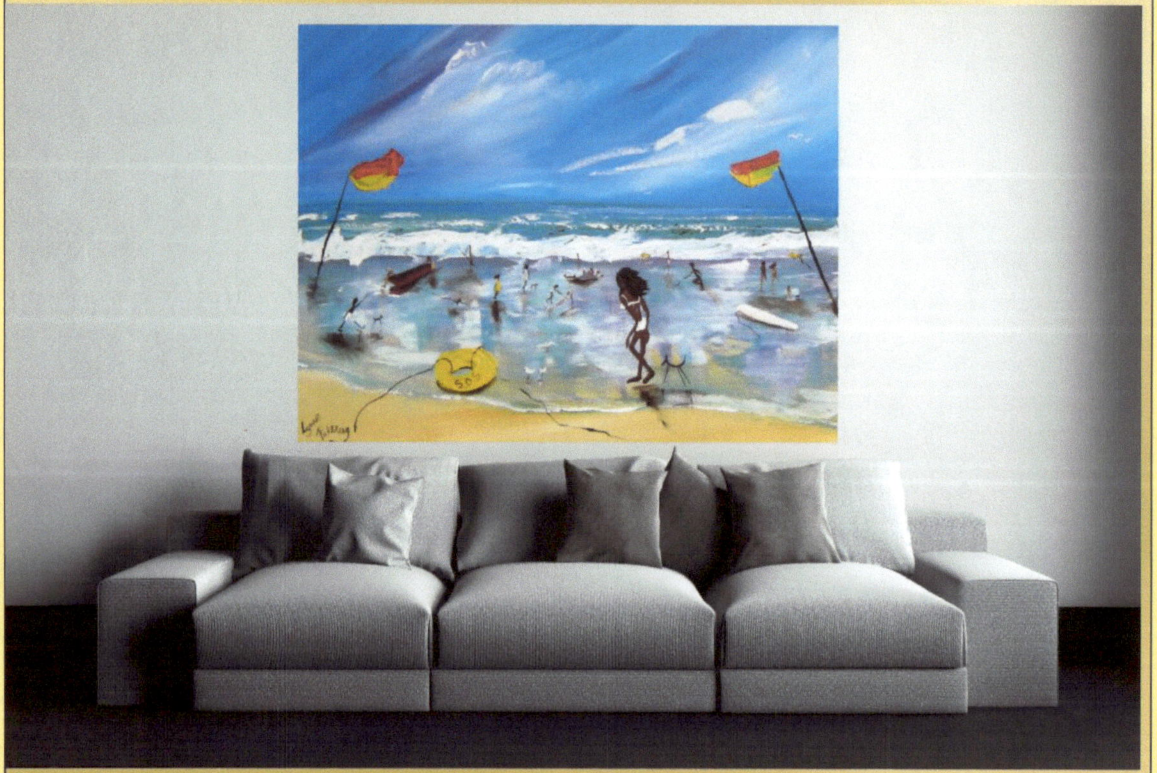

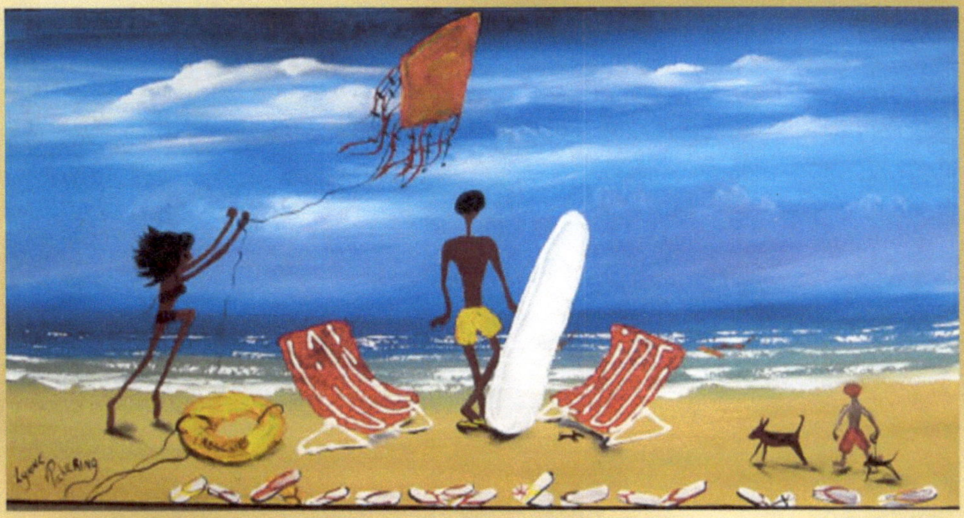

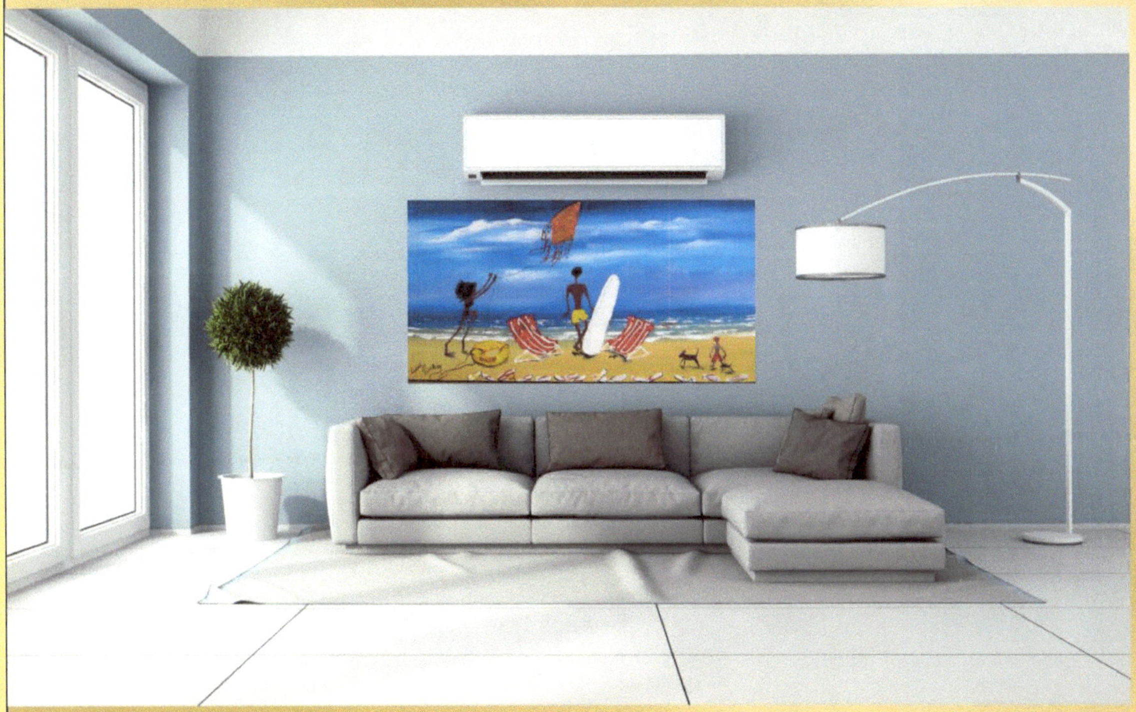

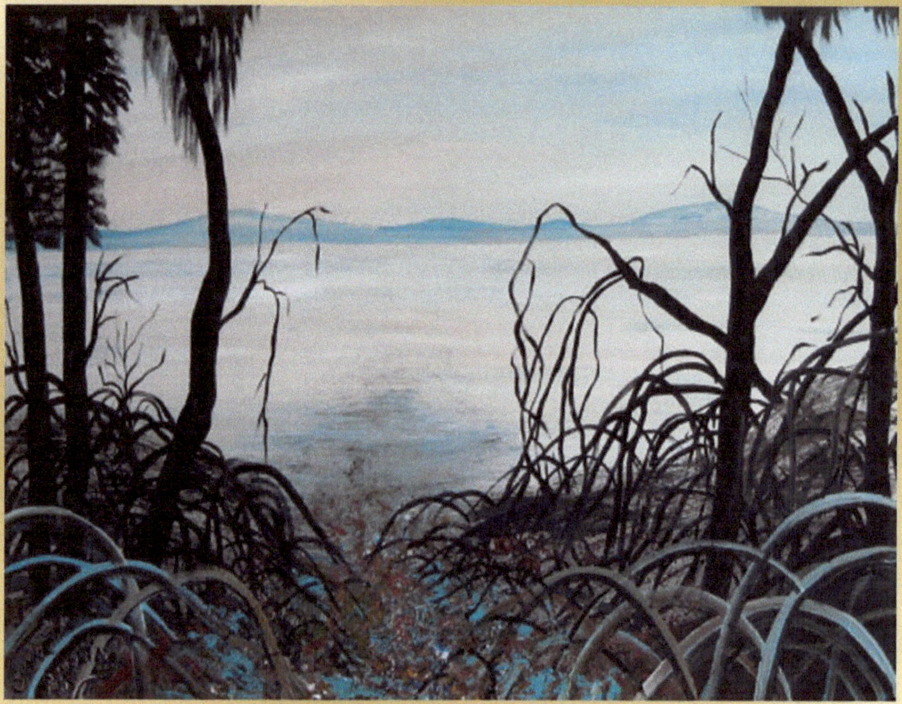

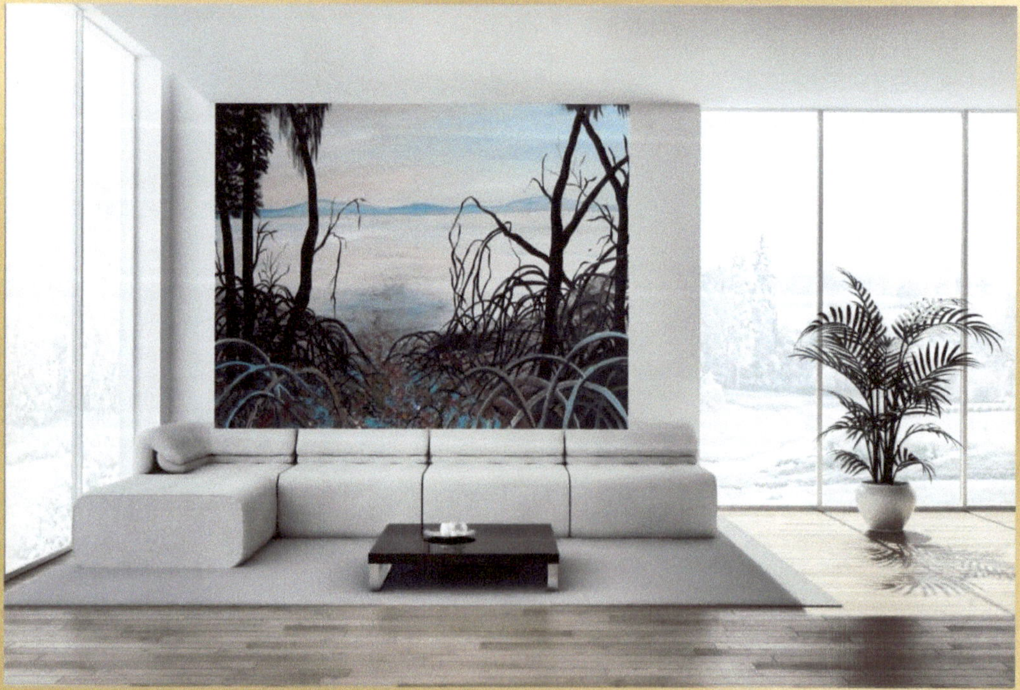

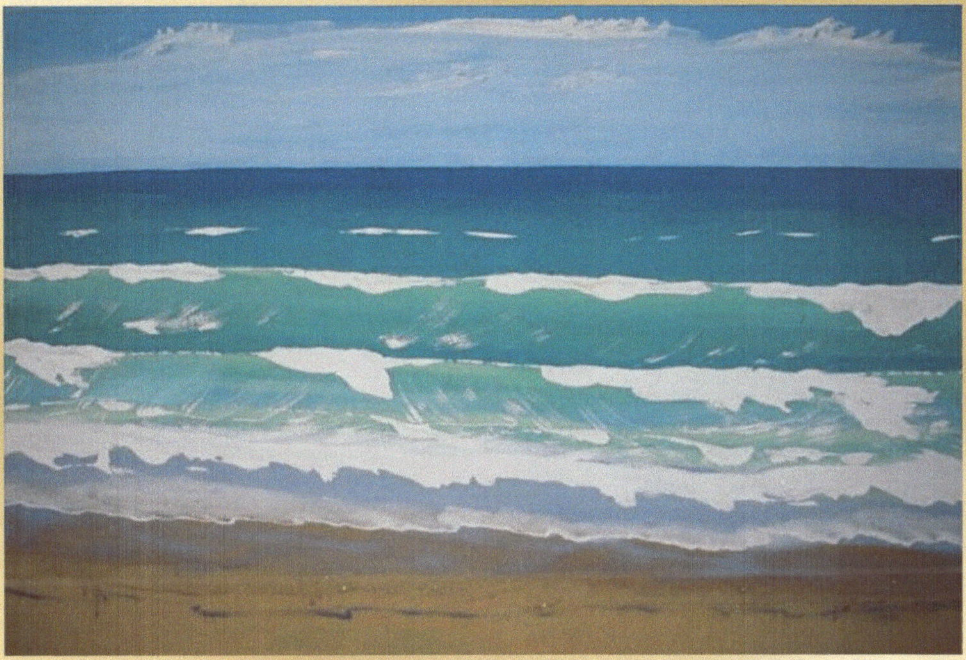

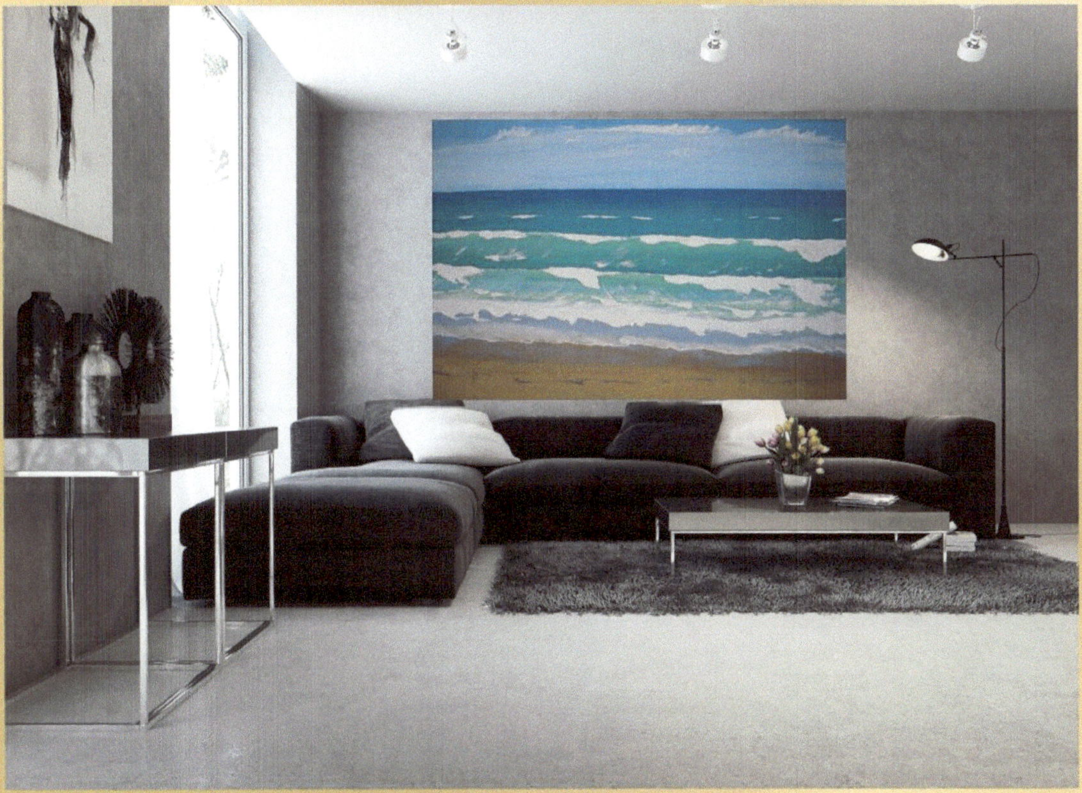

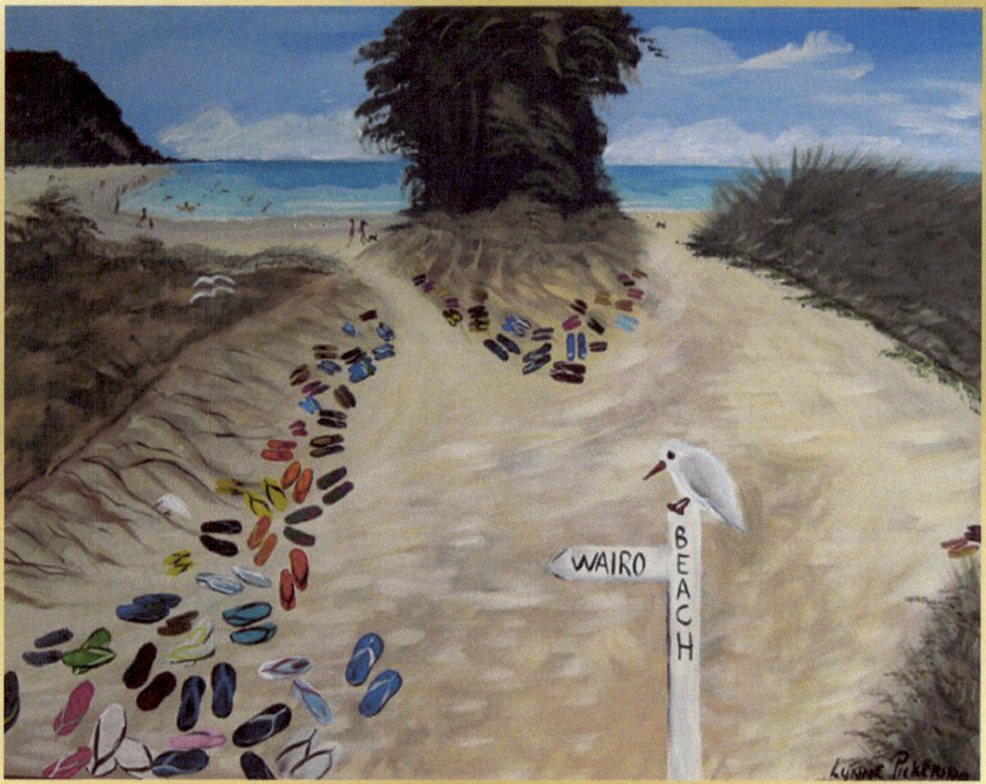
WAIRO
BEACH

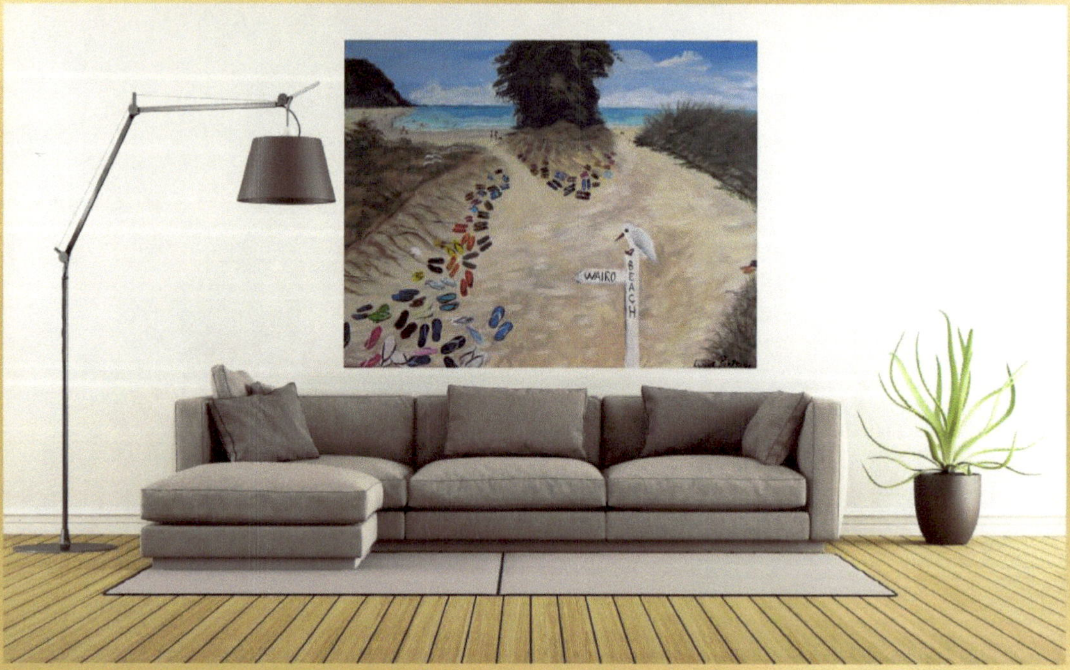
WAIRO
BEACH

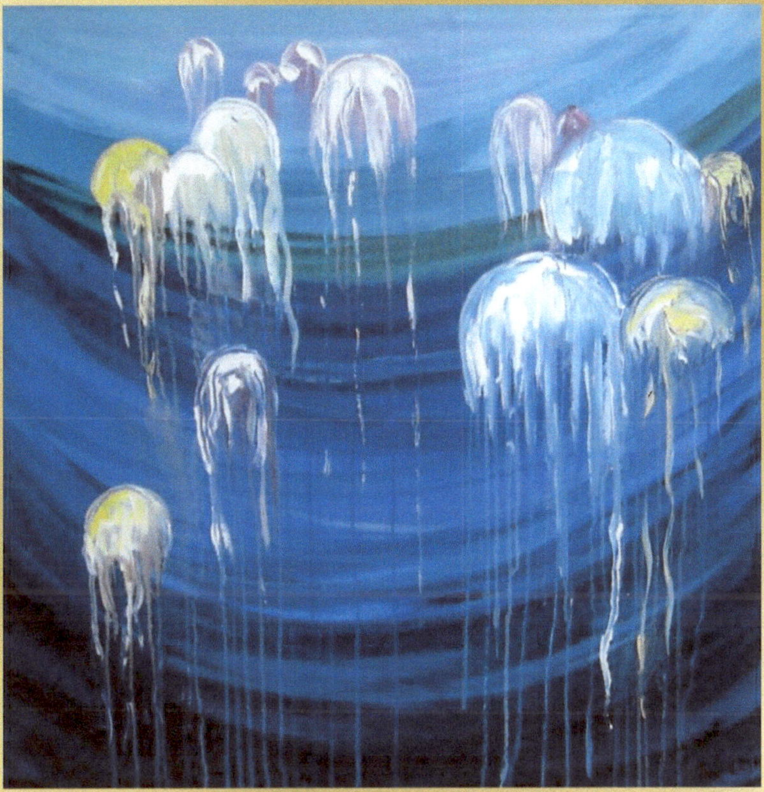

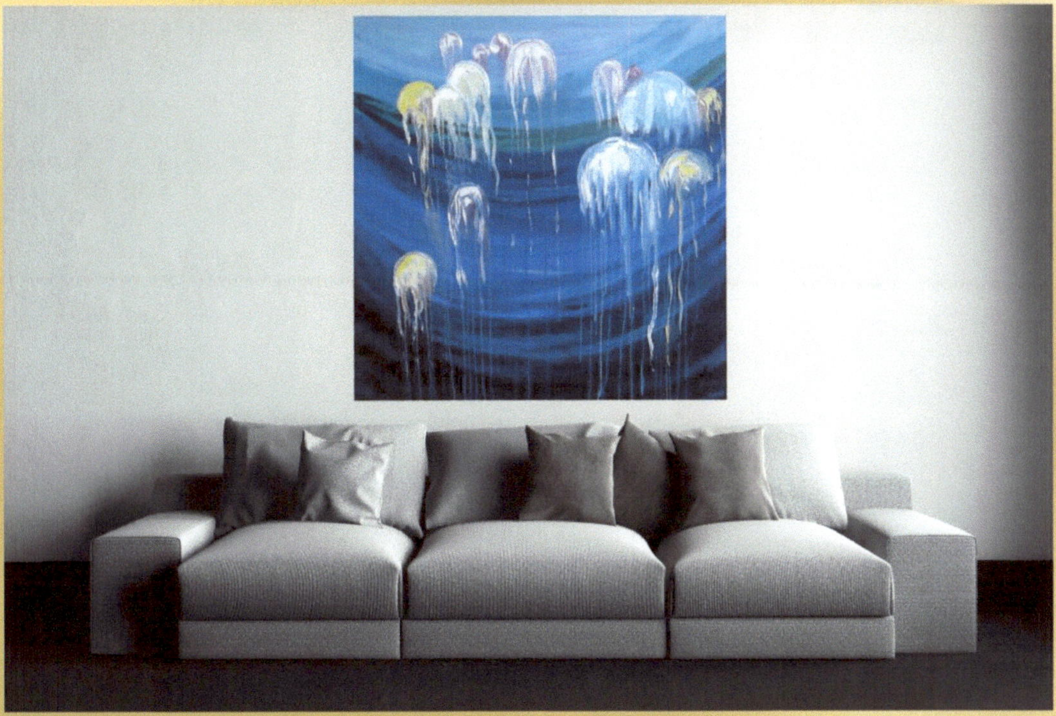

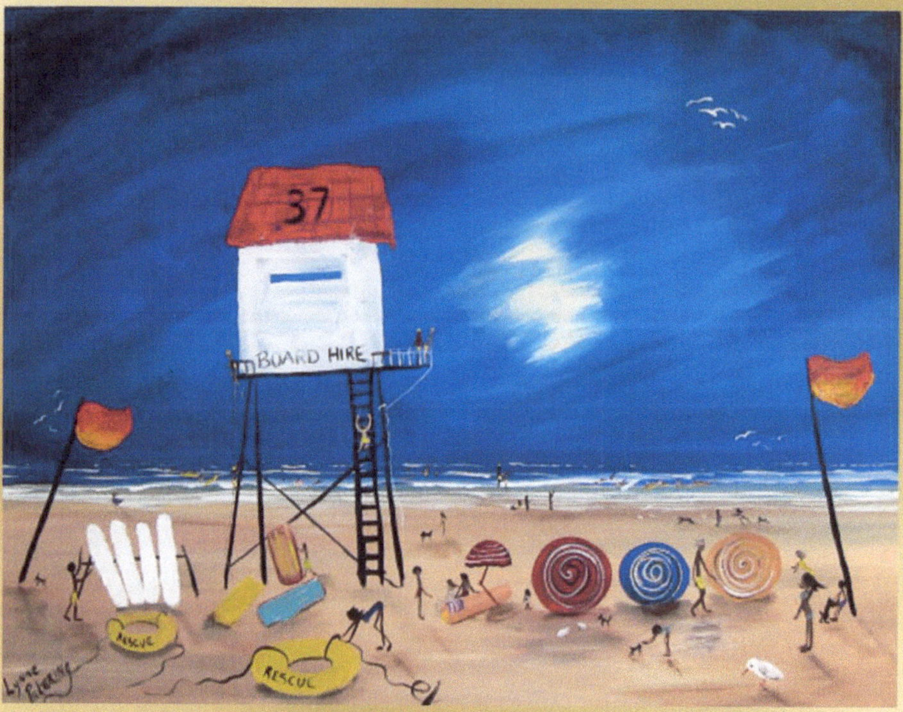
37
BOARD HIRE
RESCUE
RESCUE

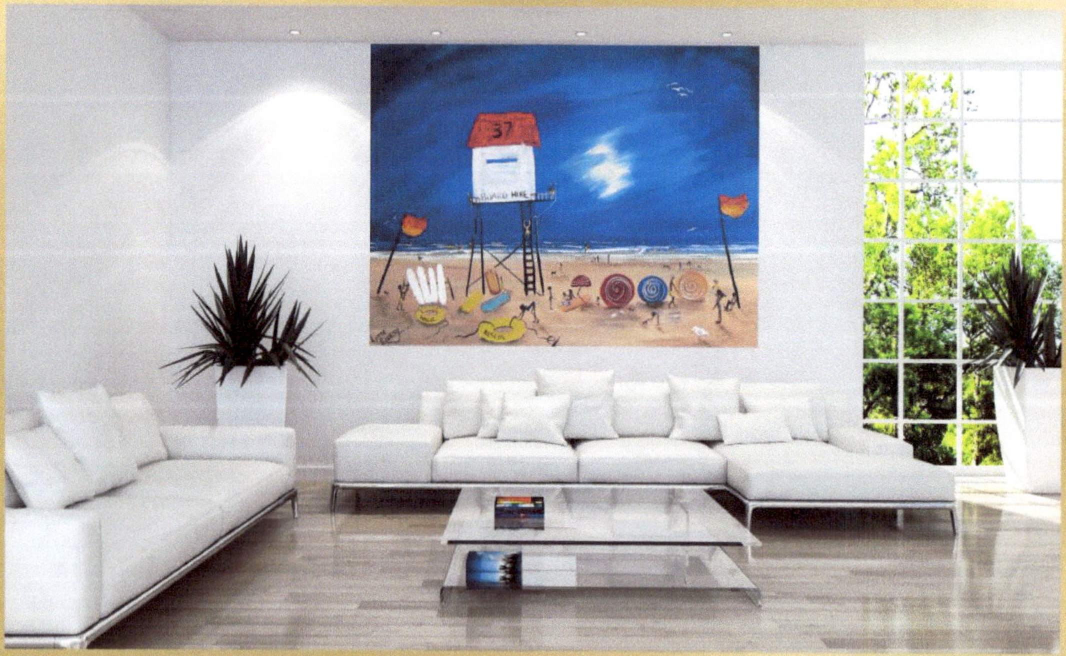

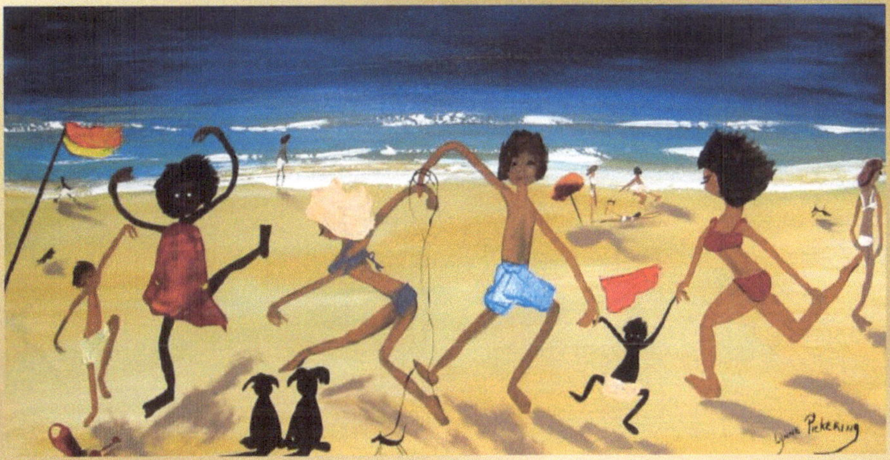

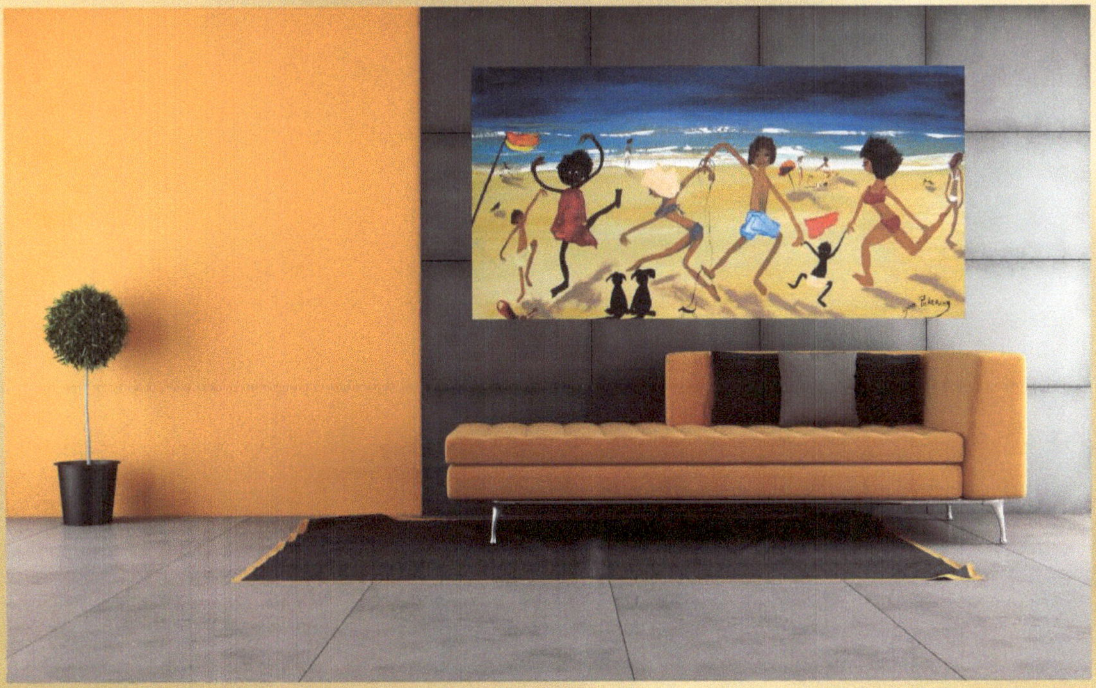

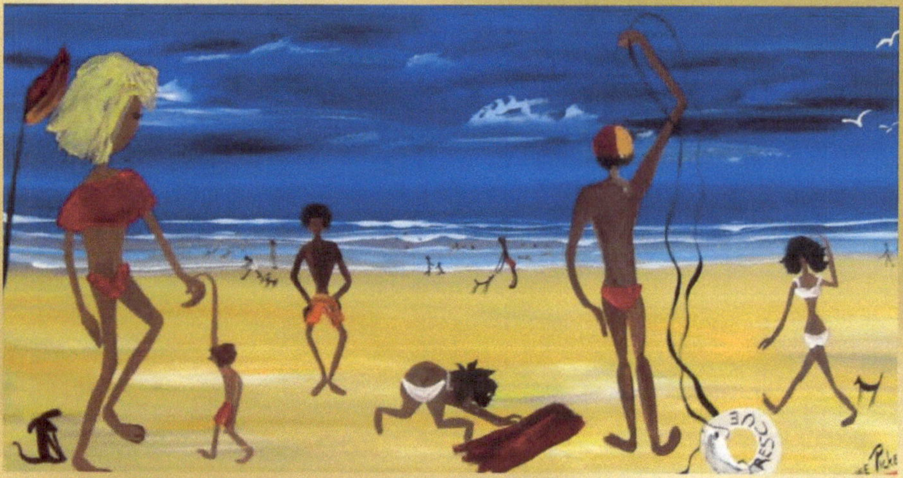

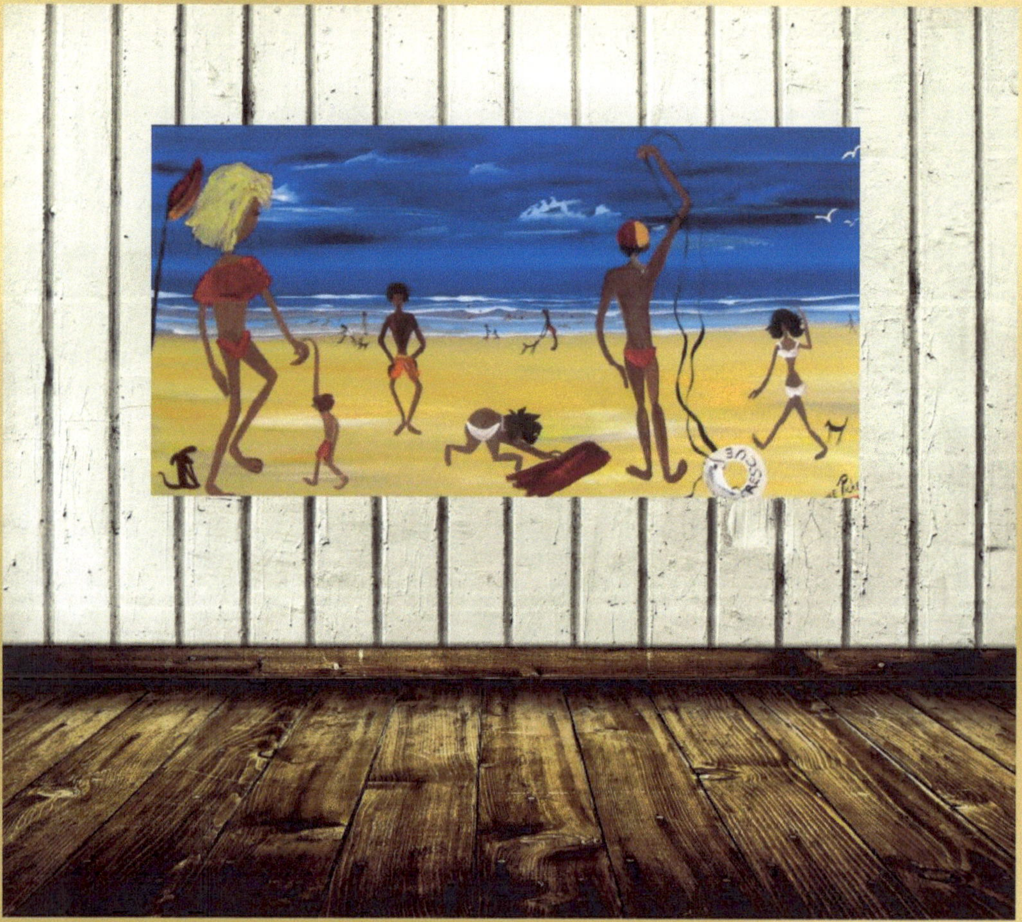

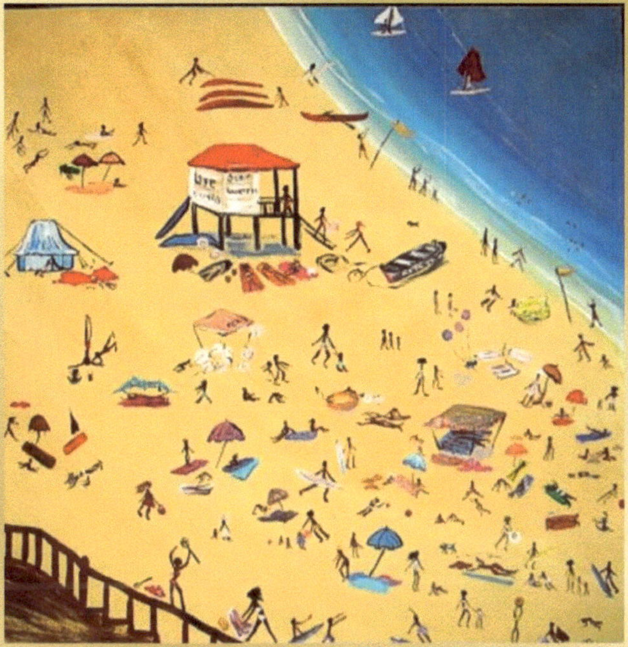

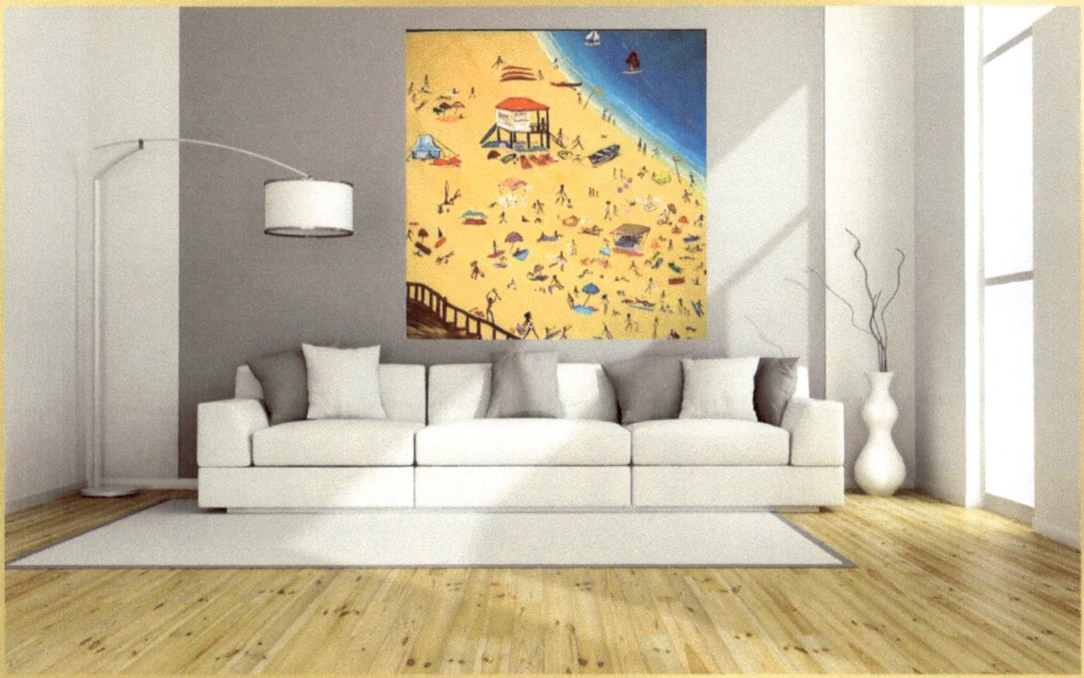

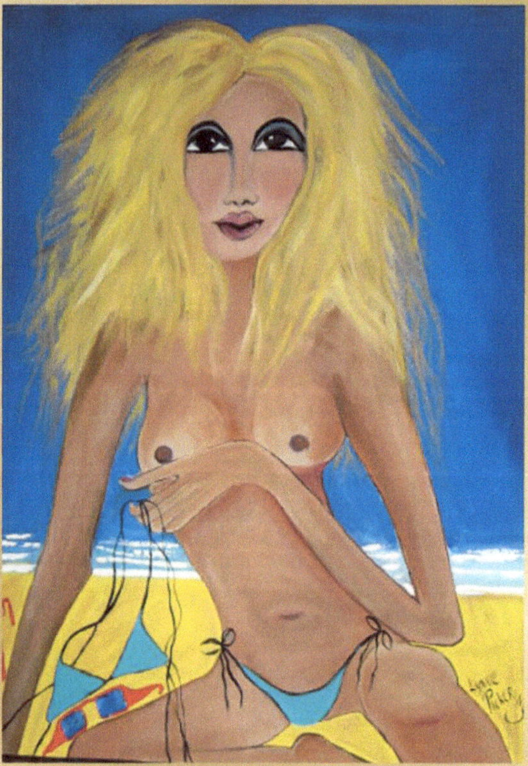

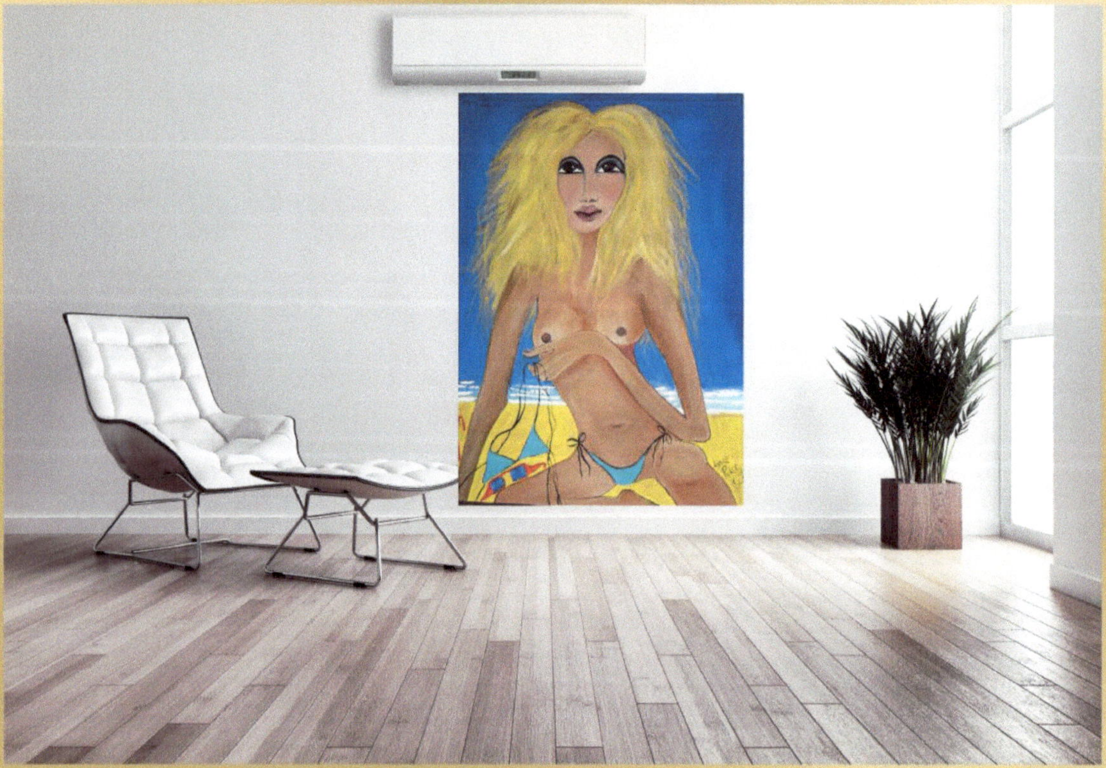

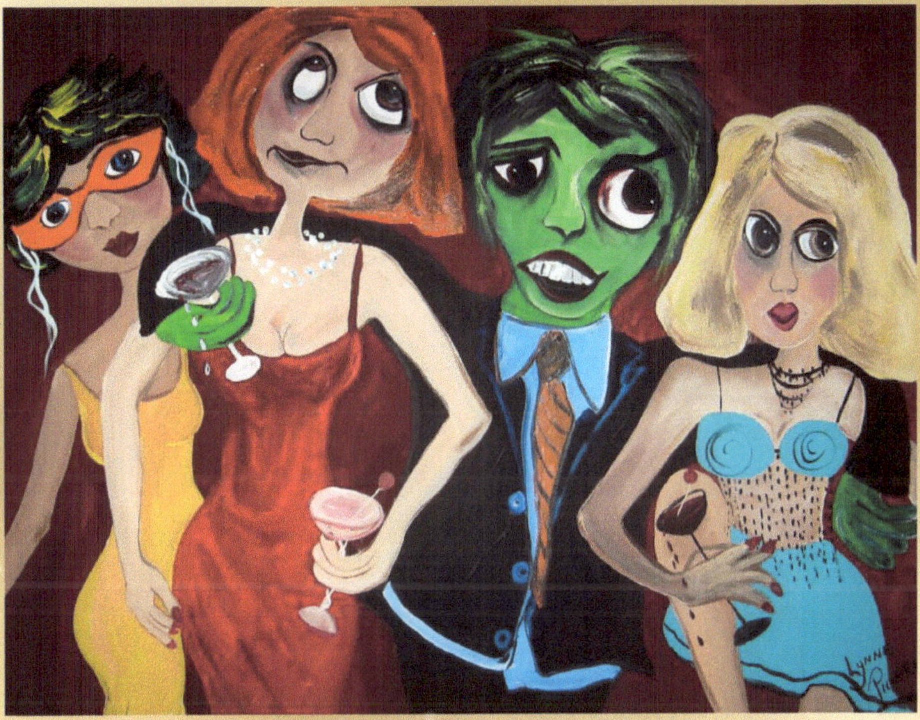

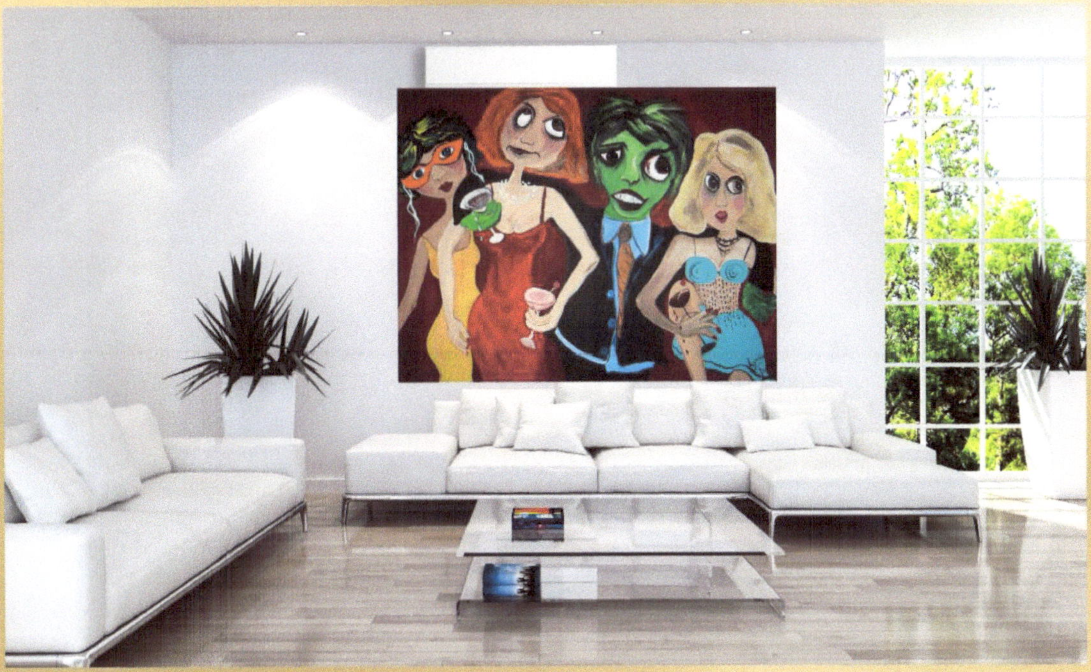

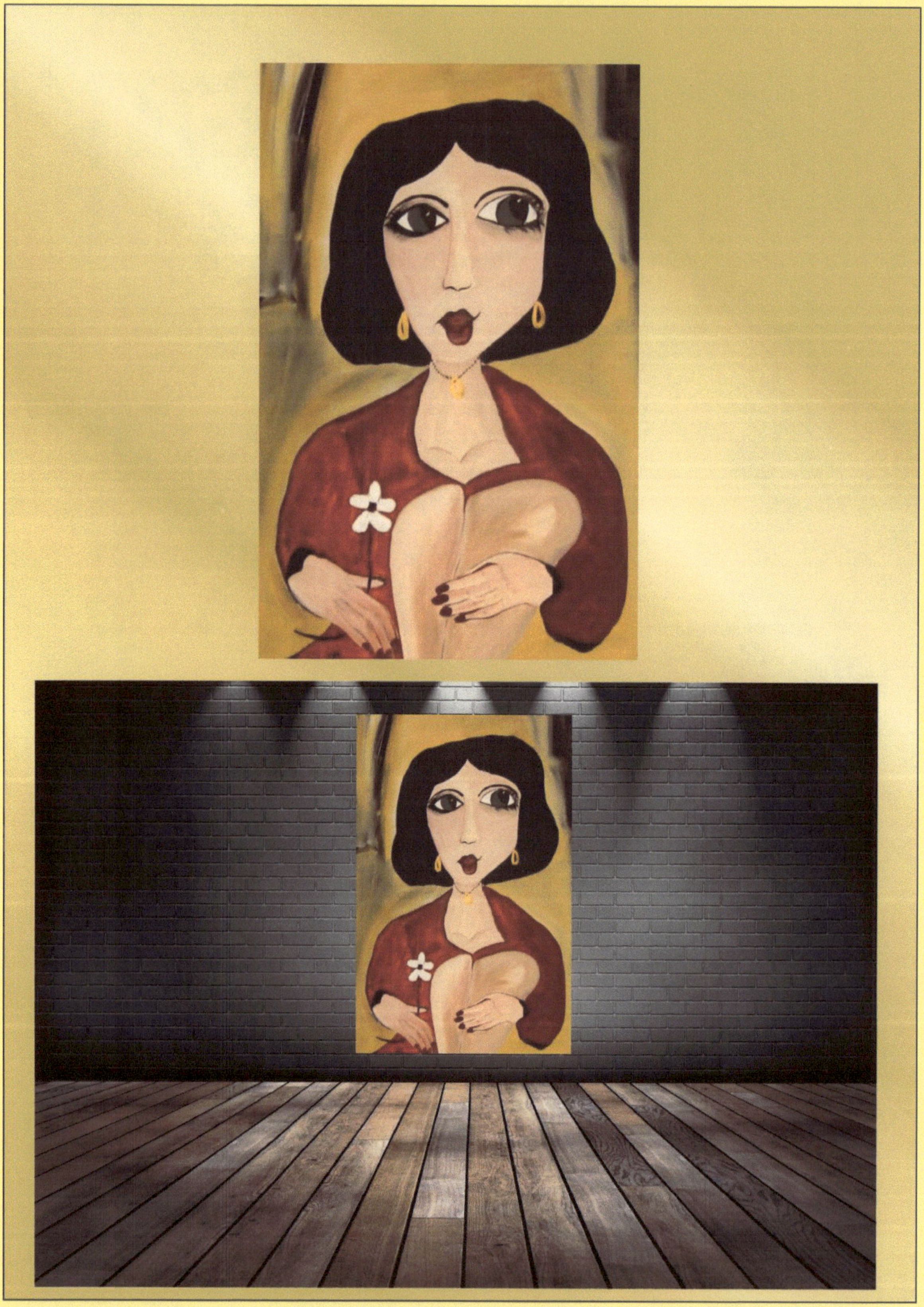

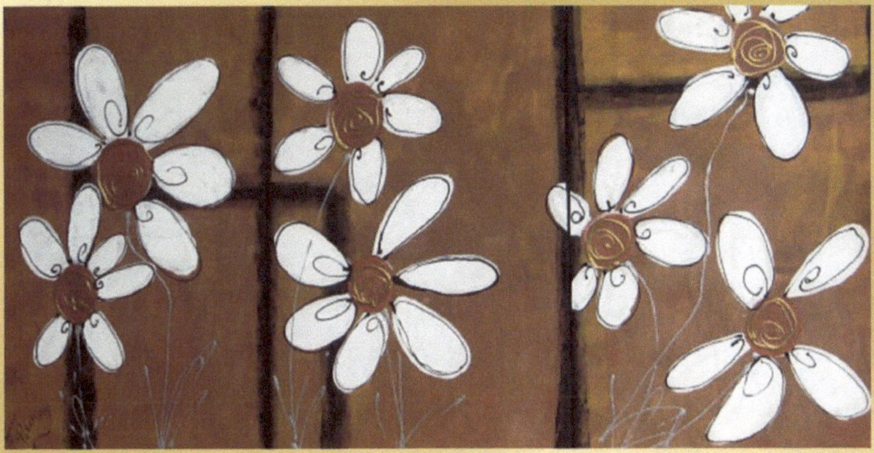

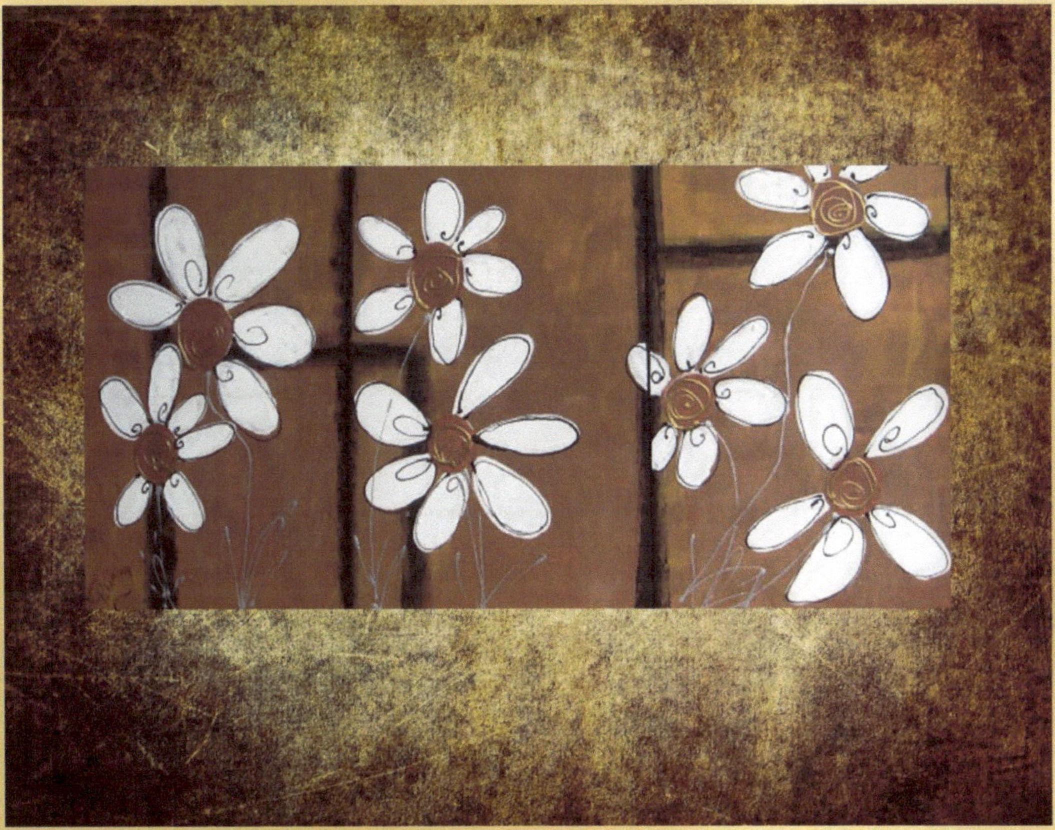

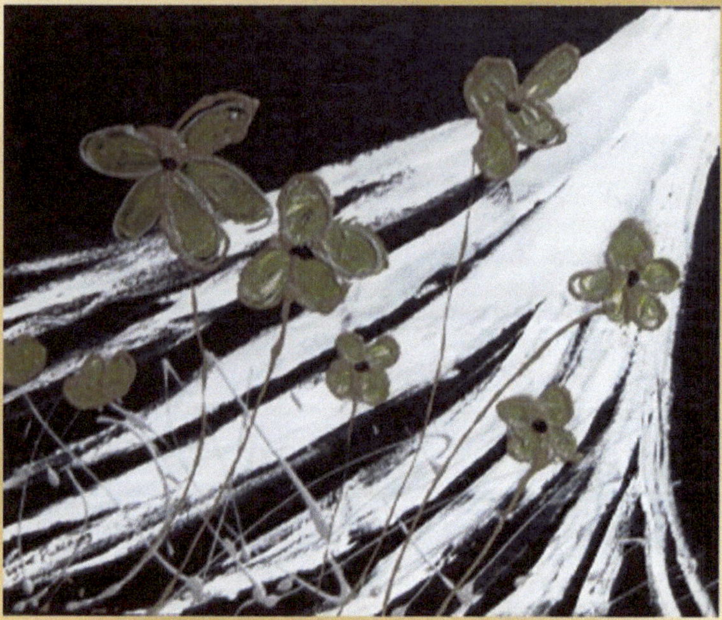

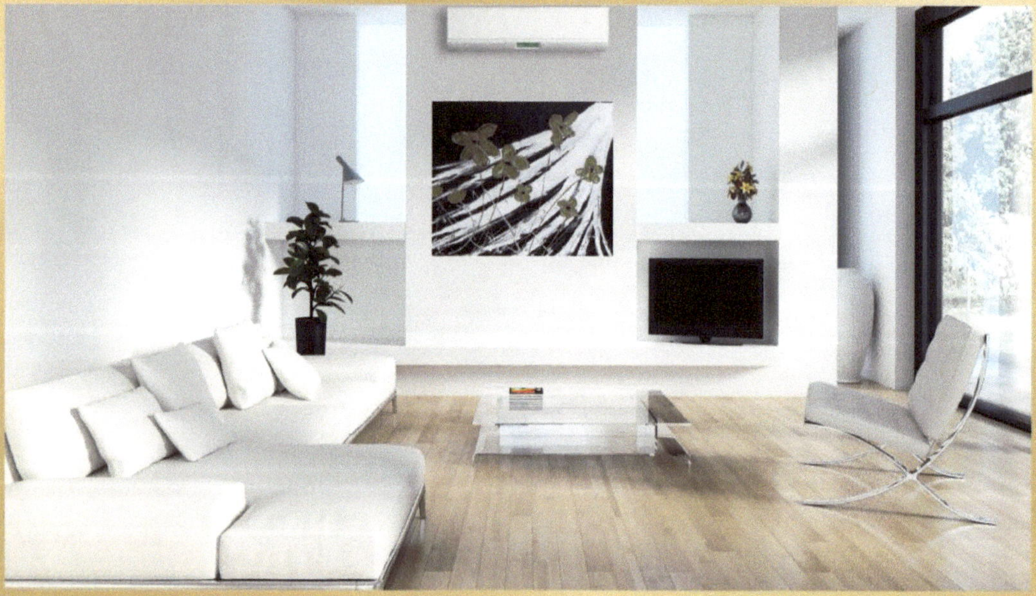

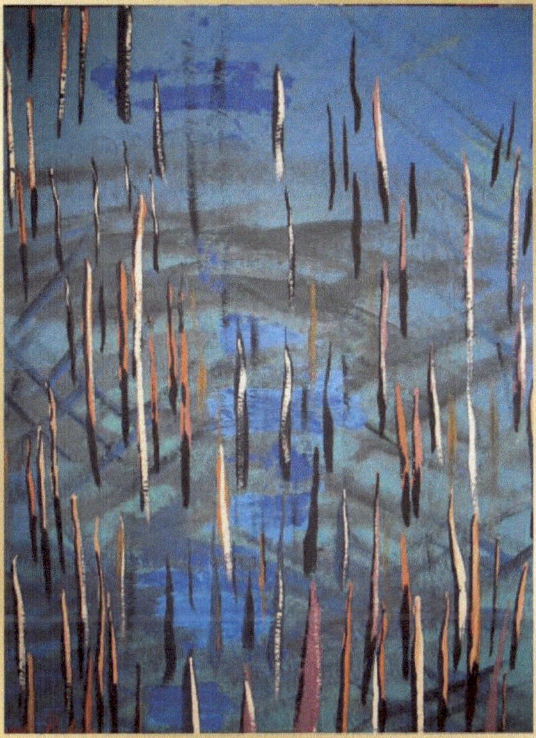

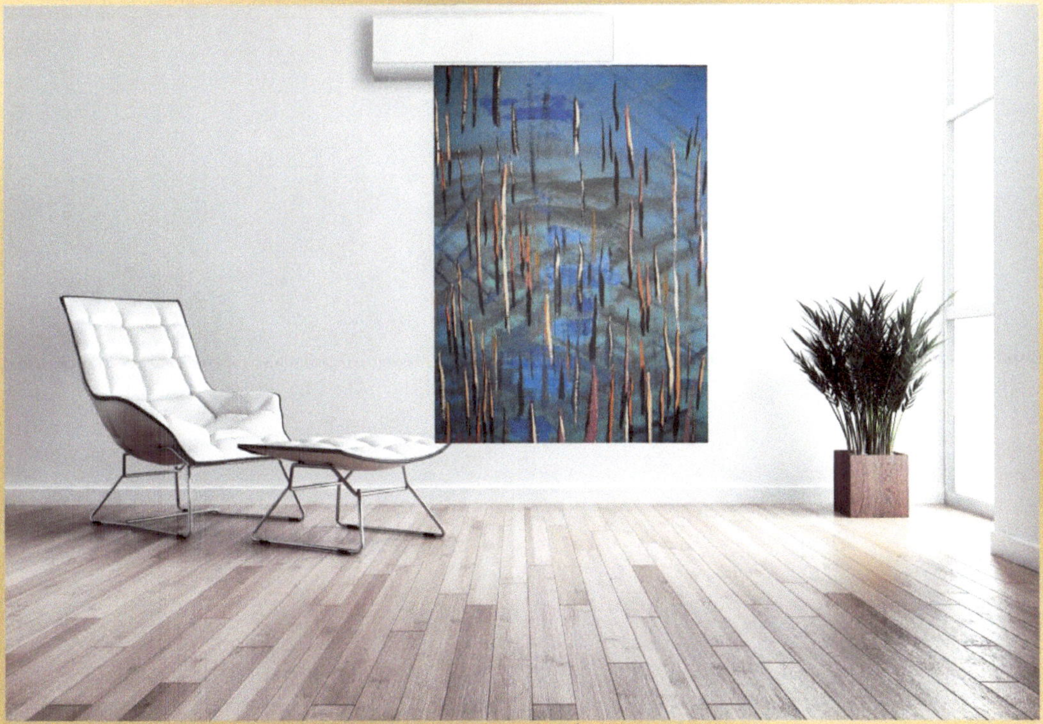

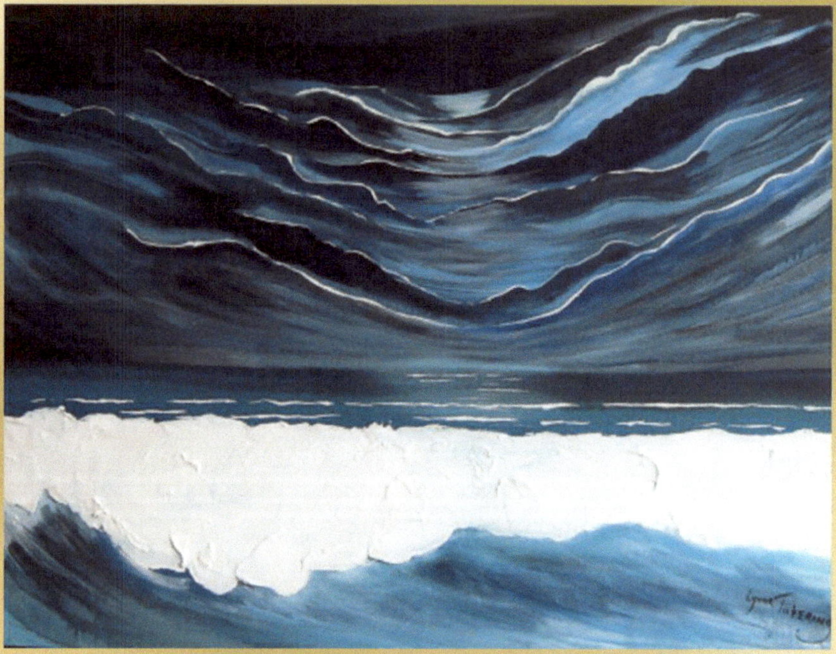

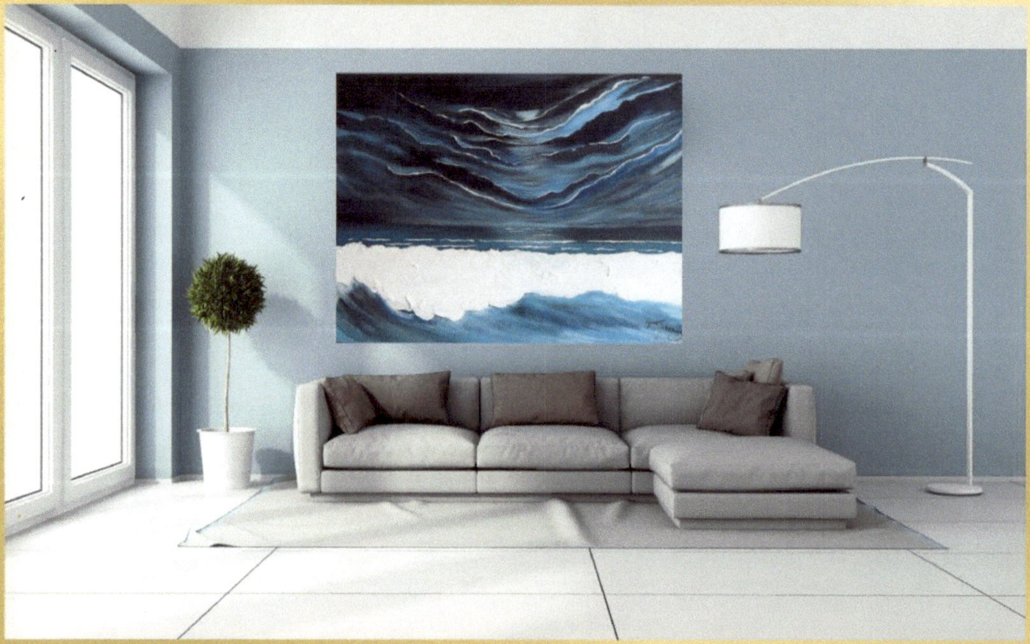

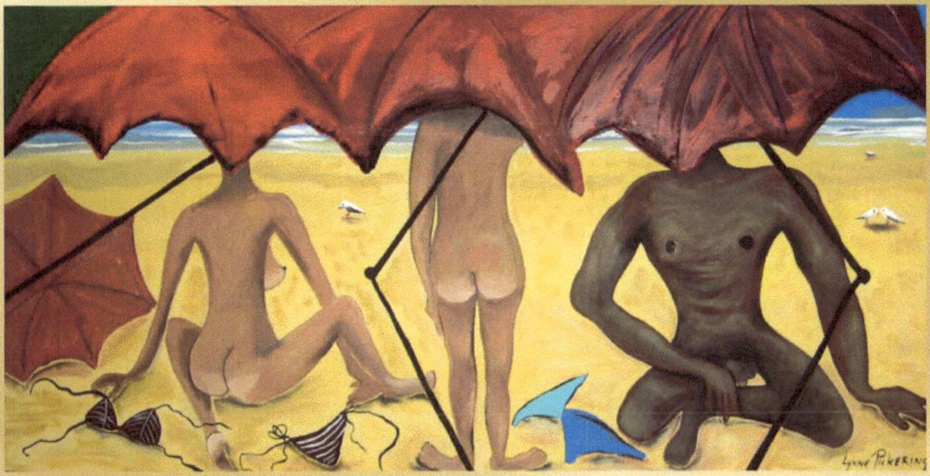

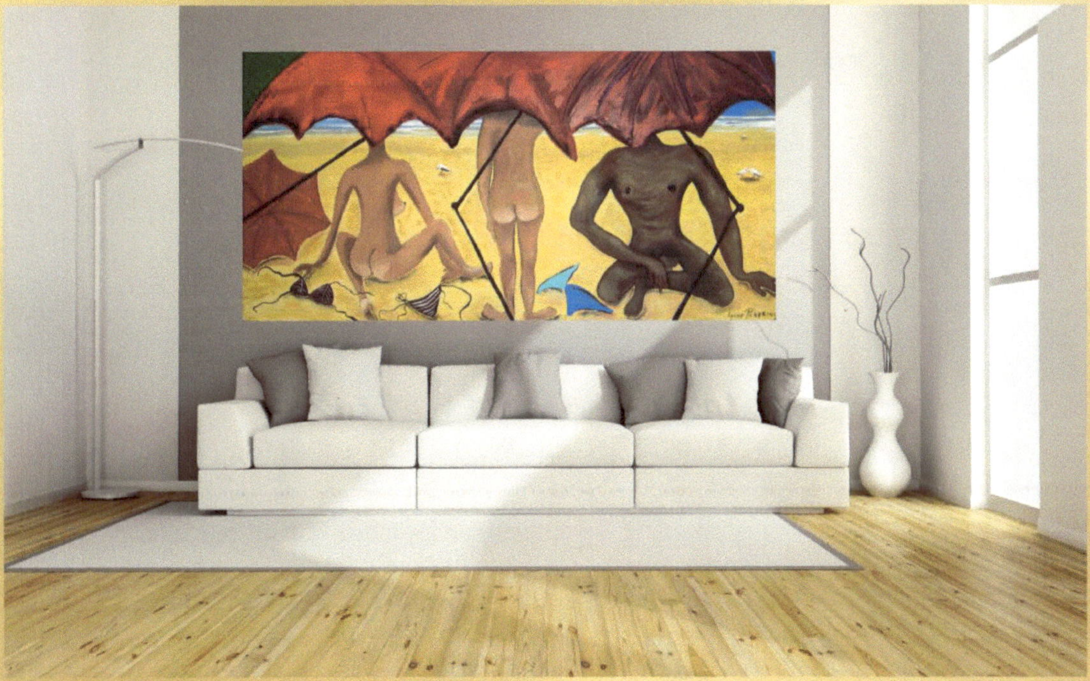

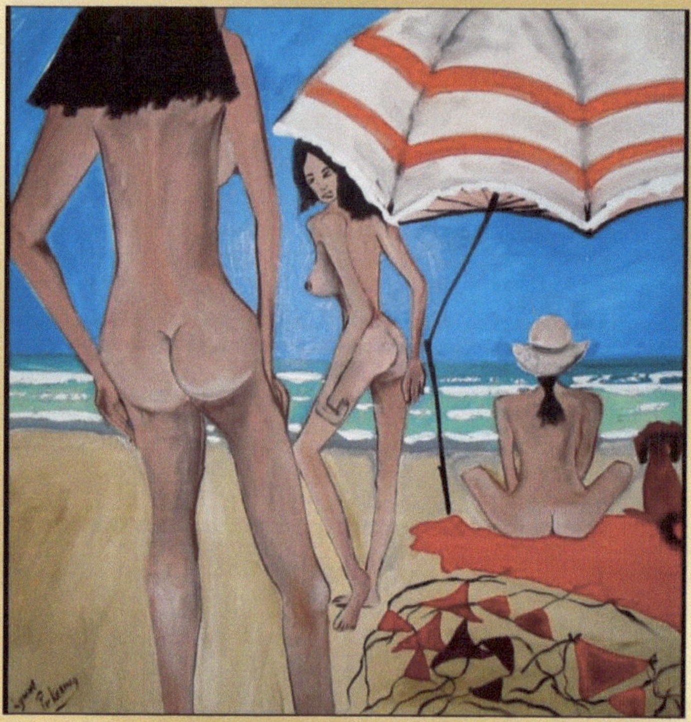

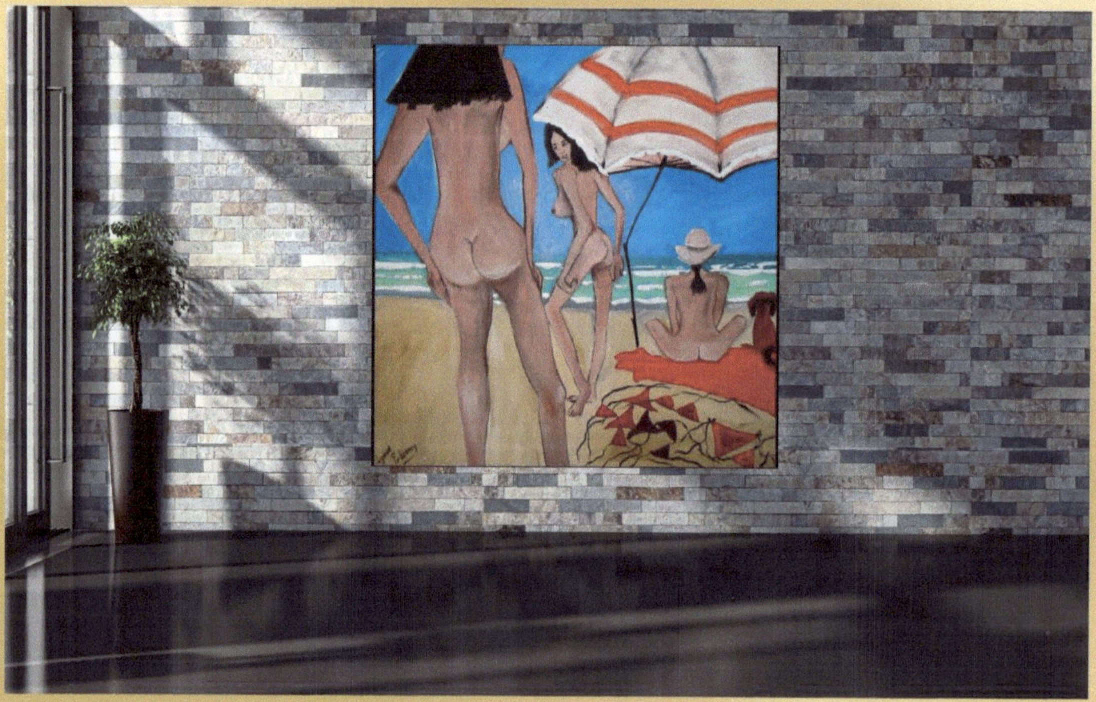

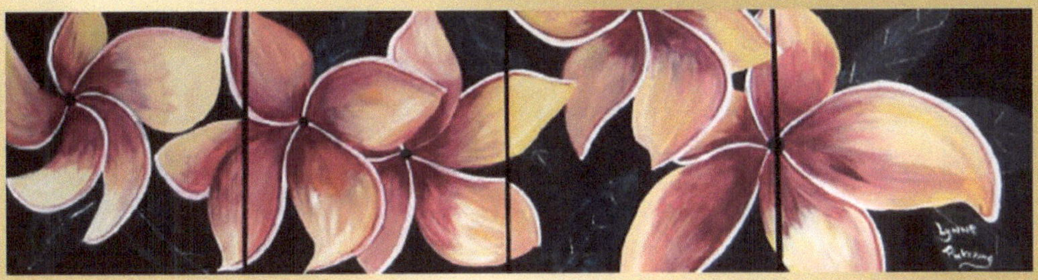

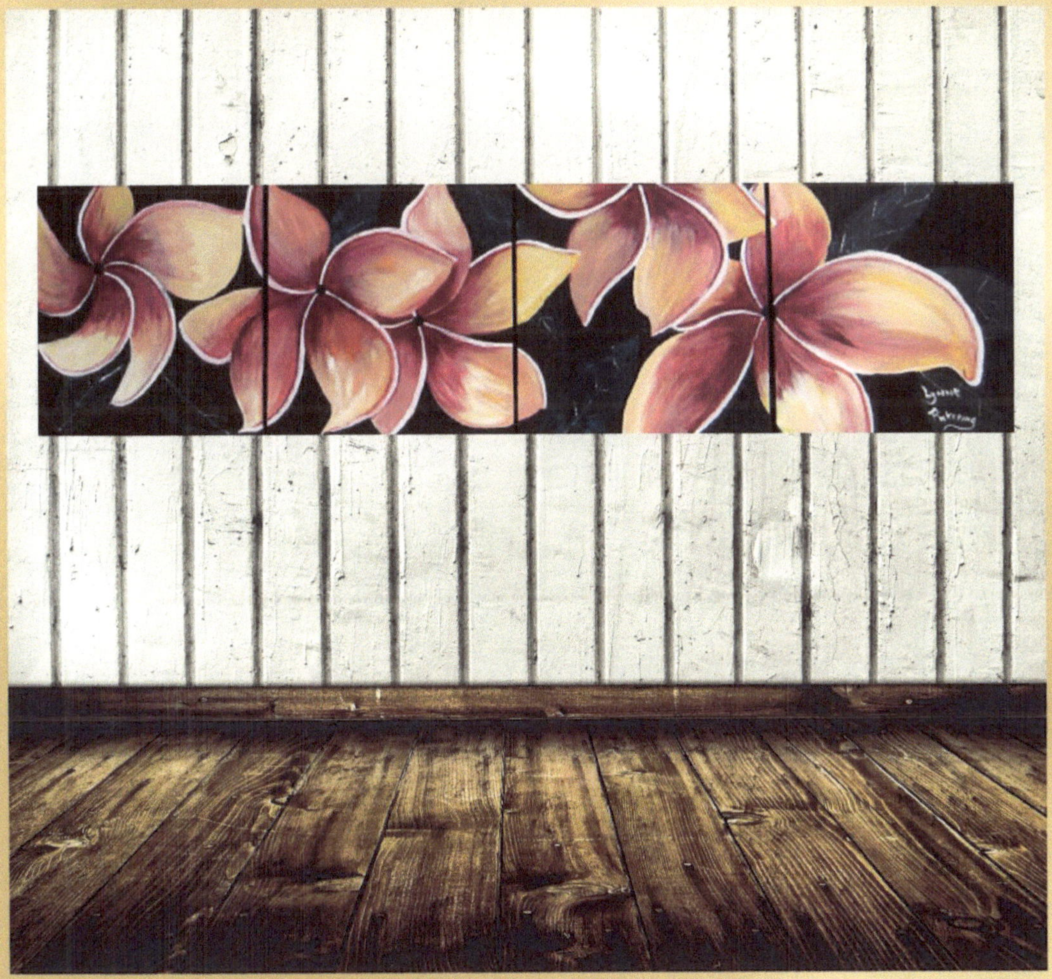

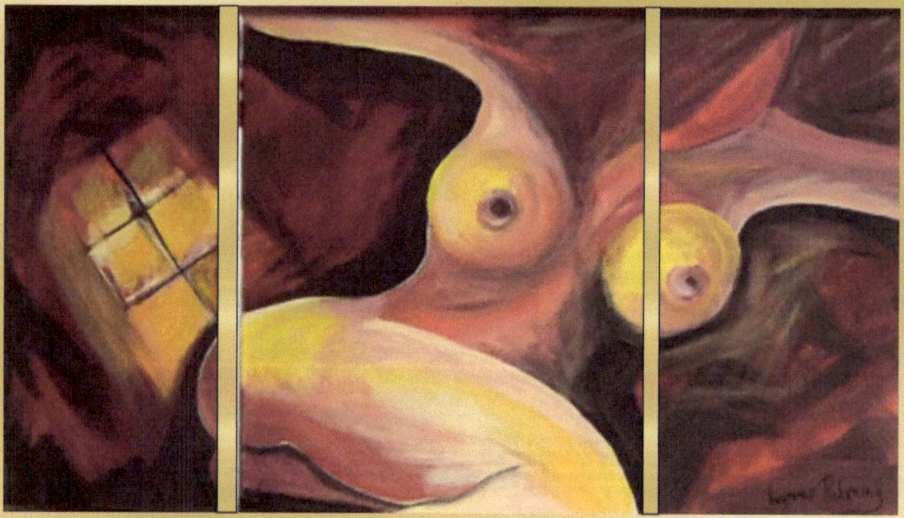

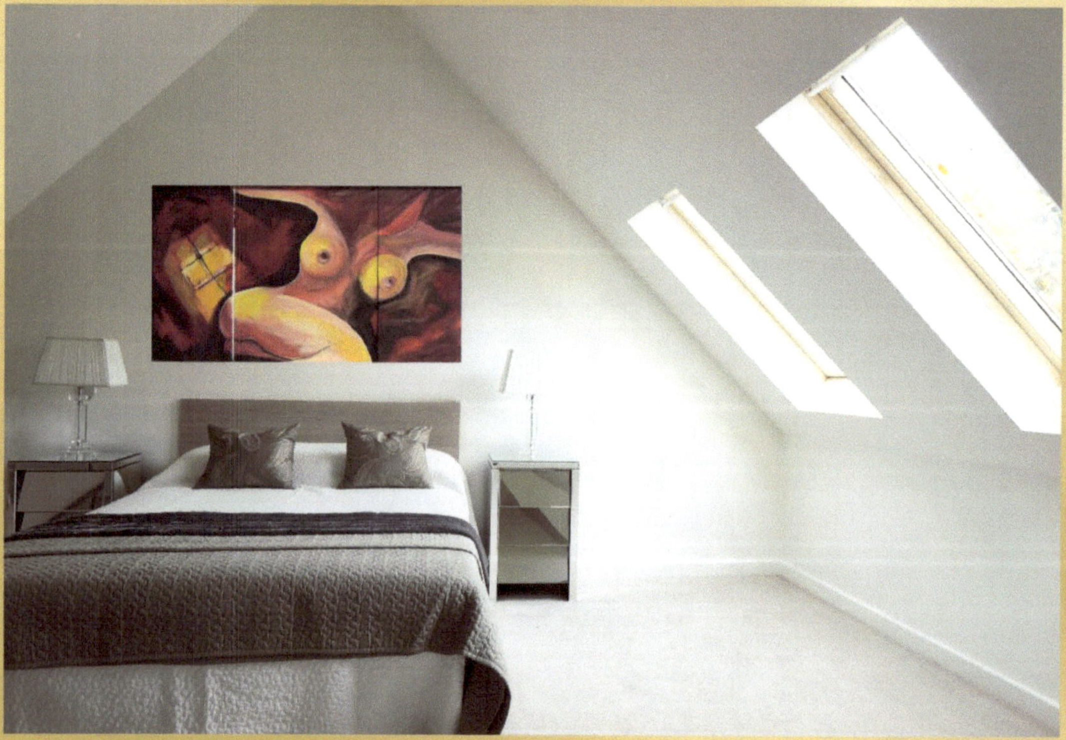

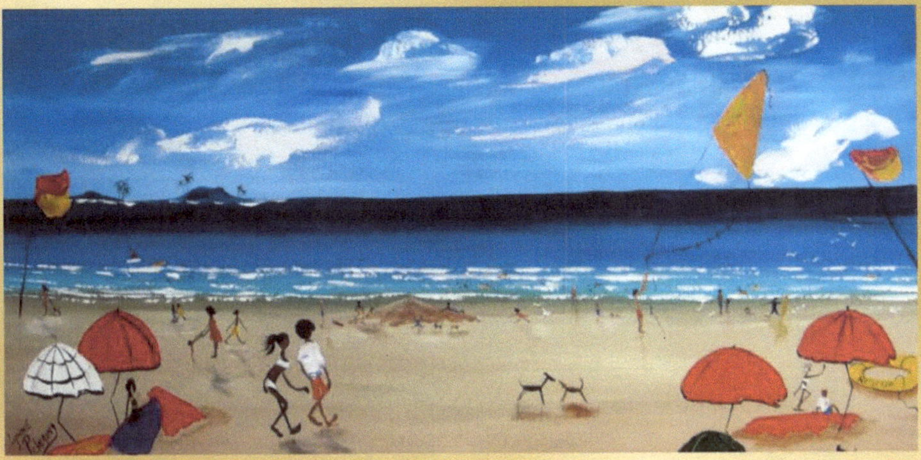

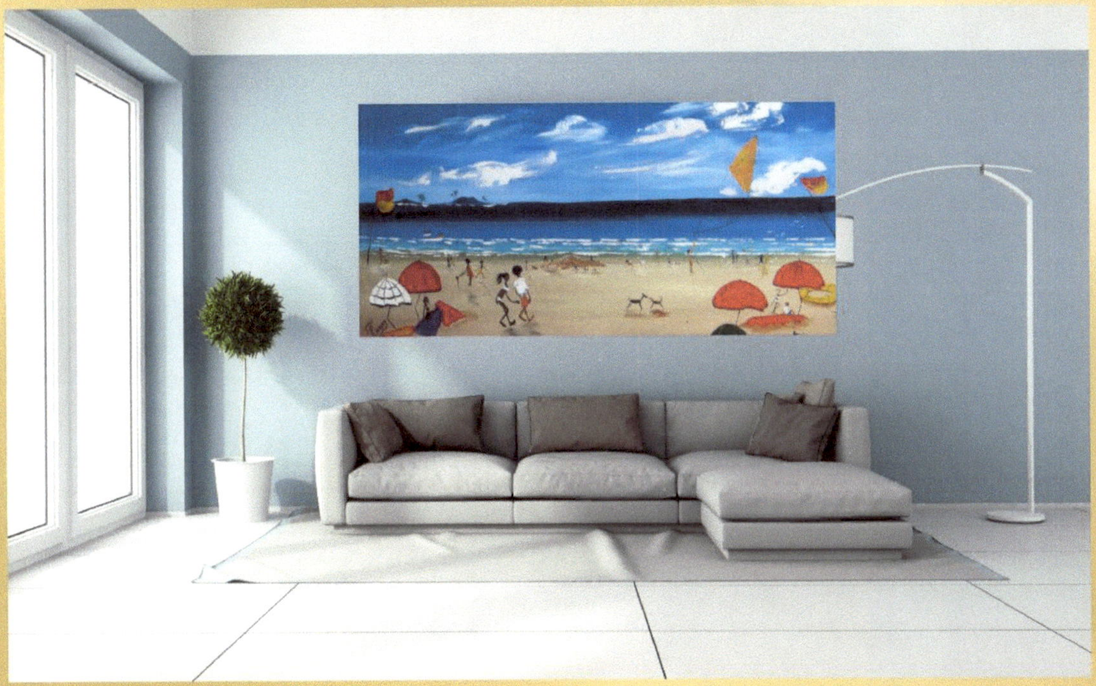

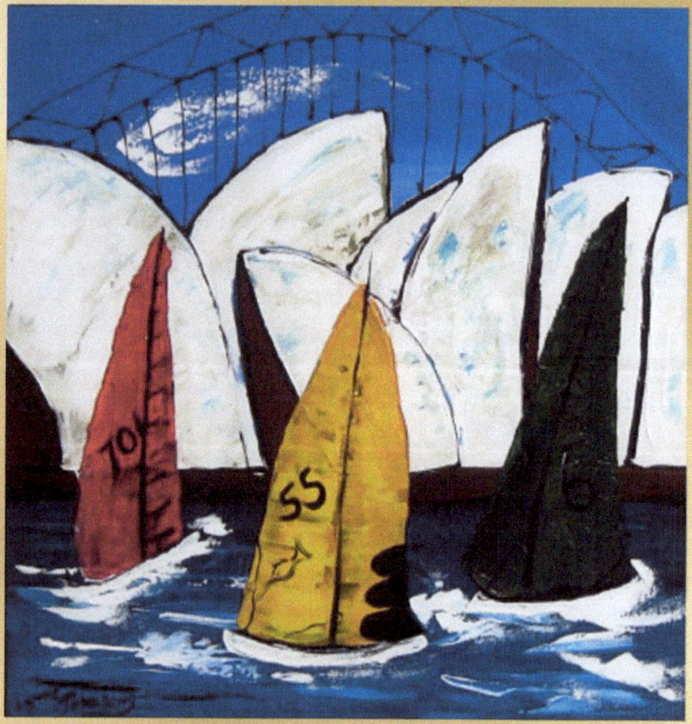
SS

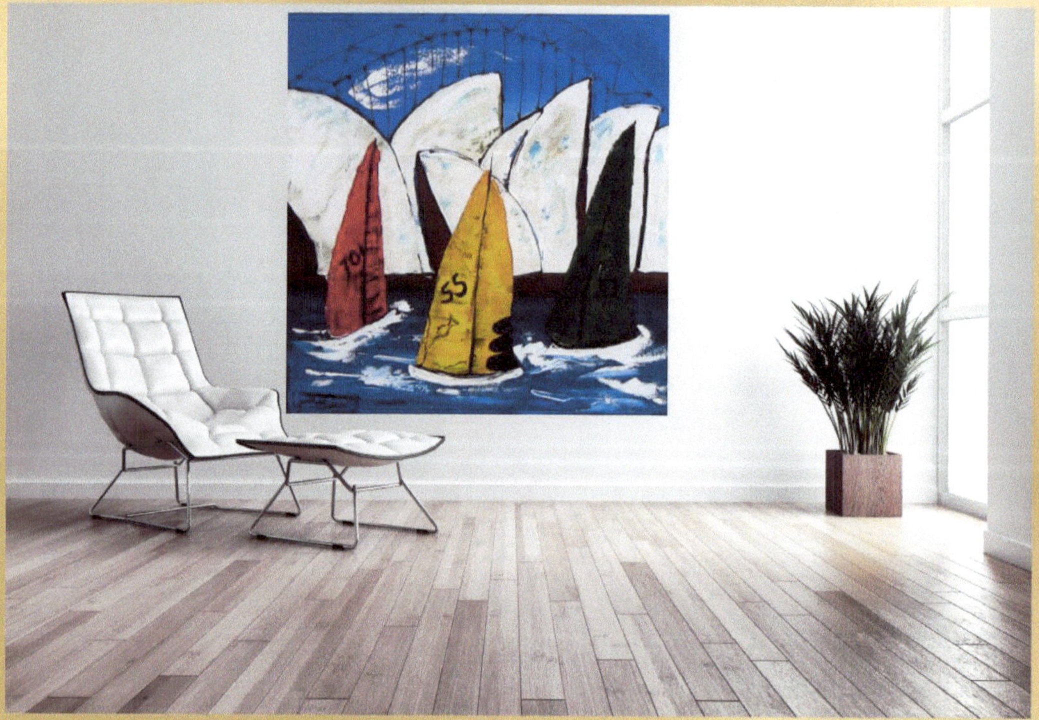

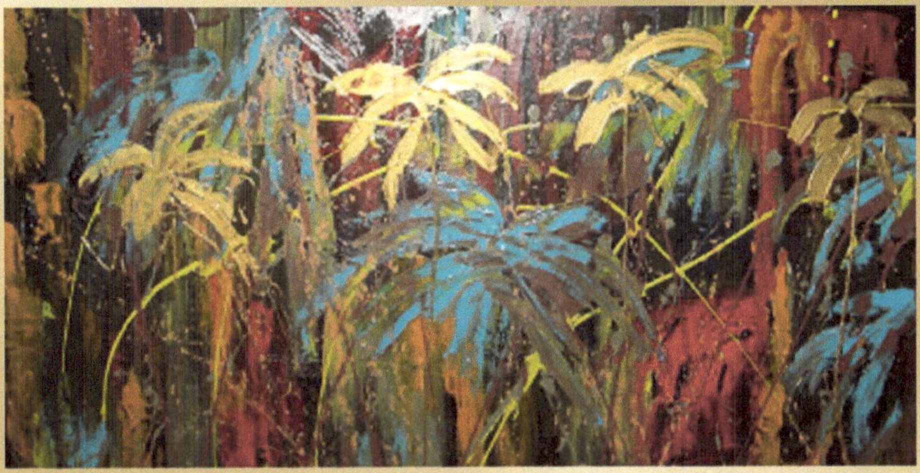

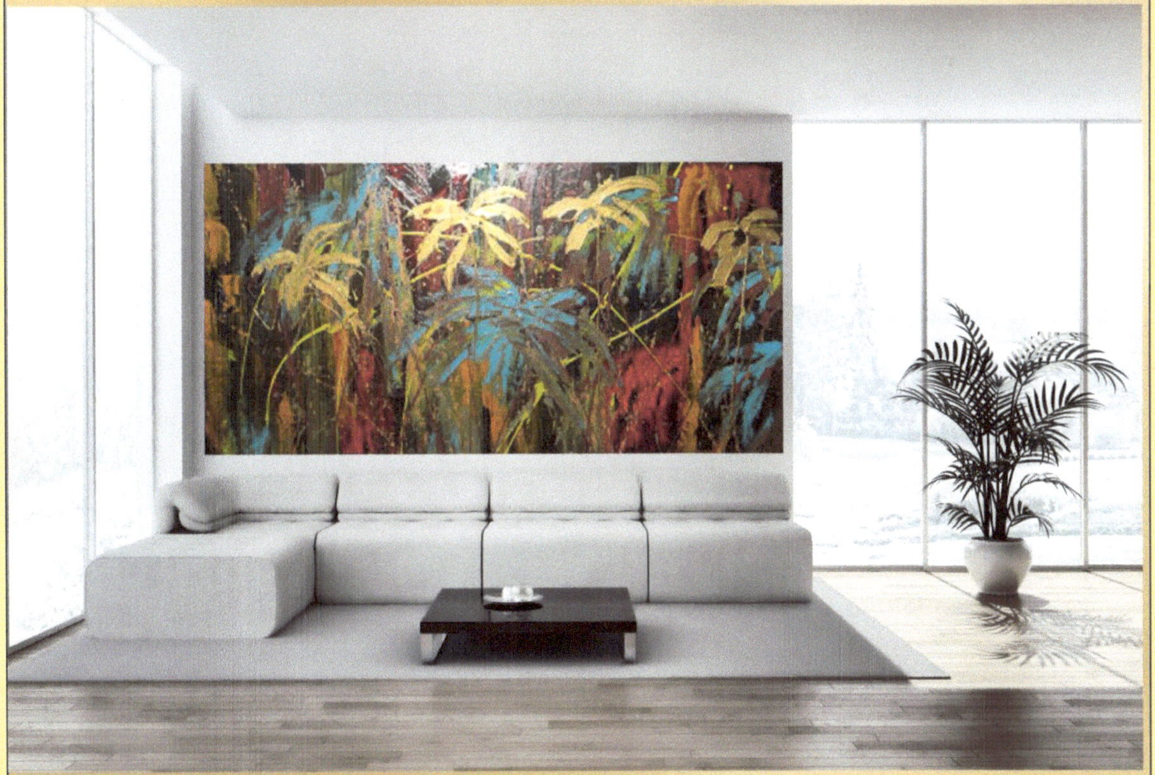

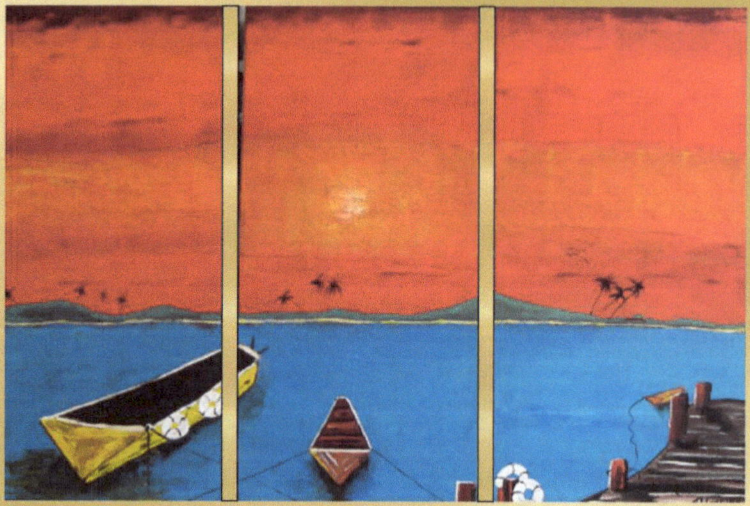

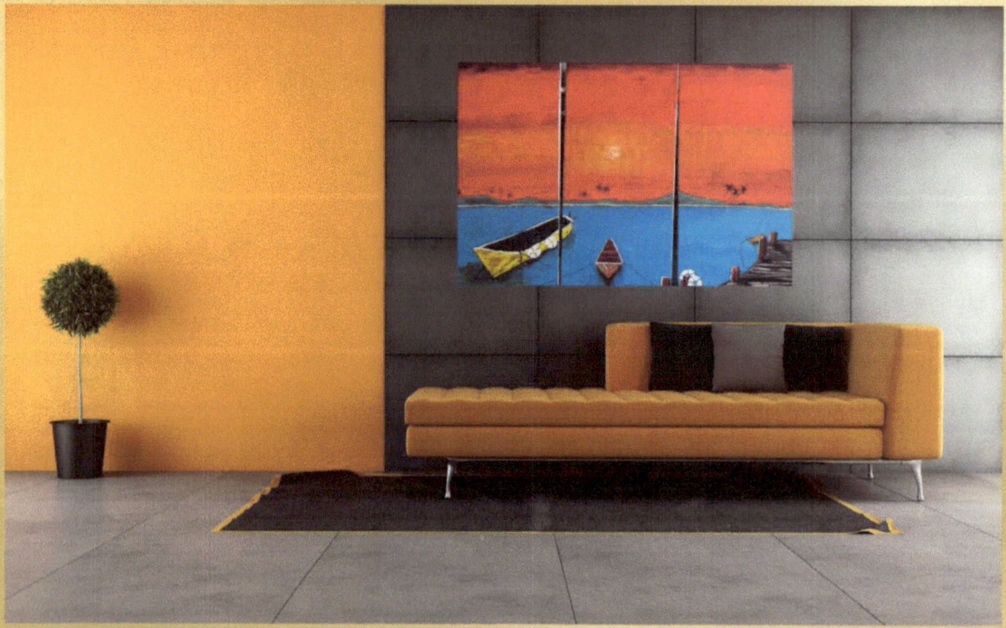

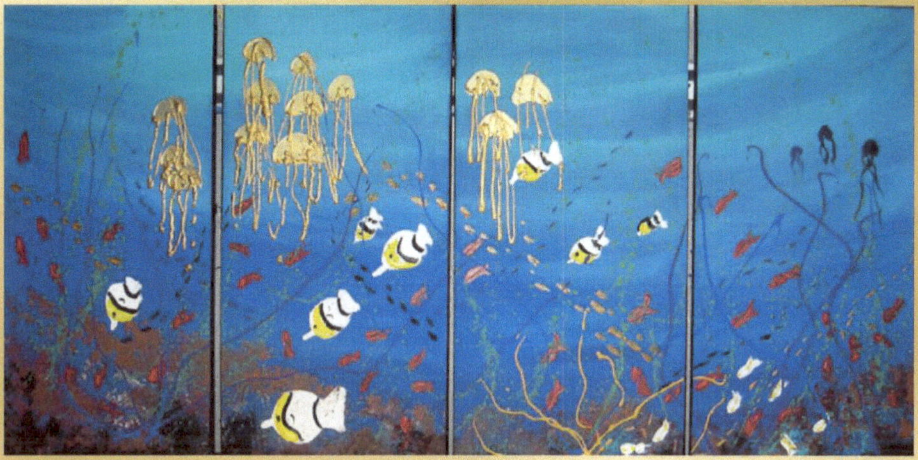

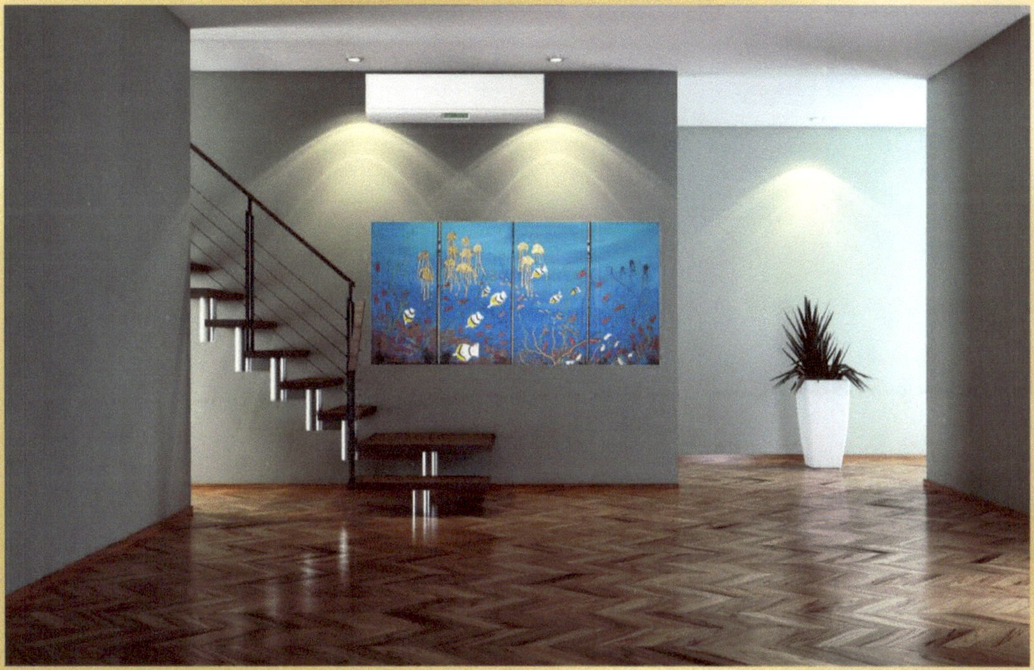

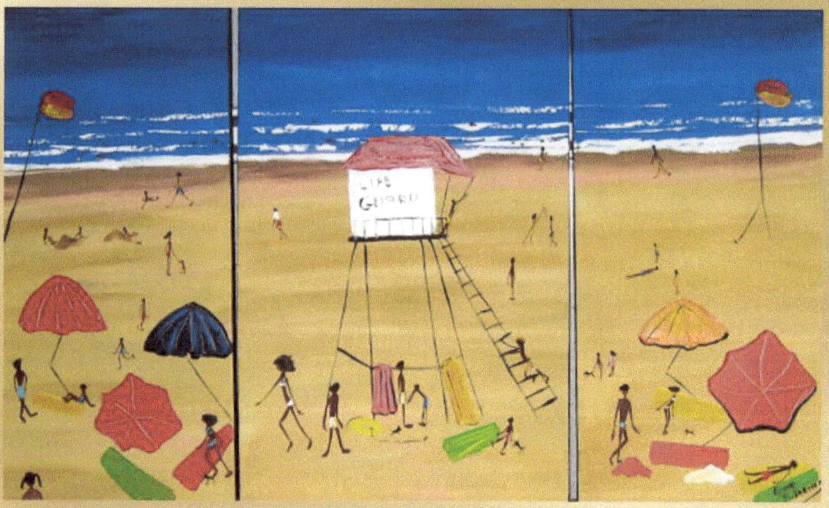

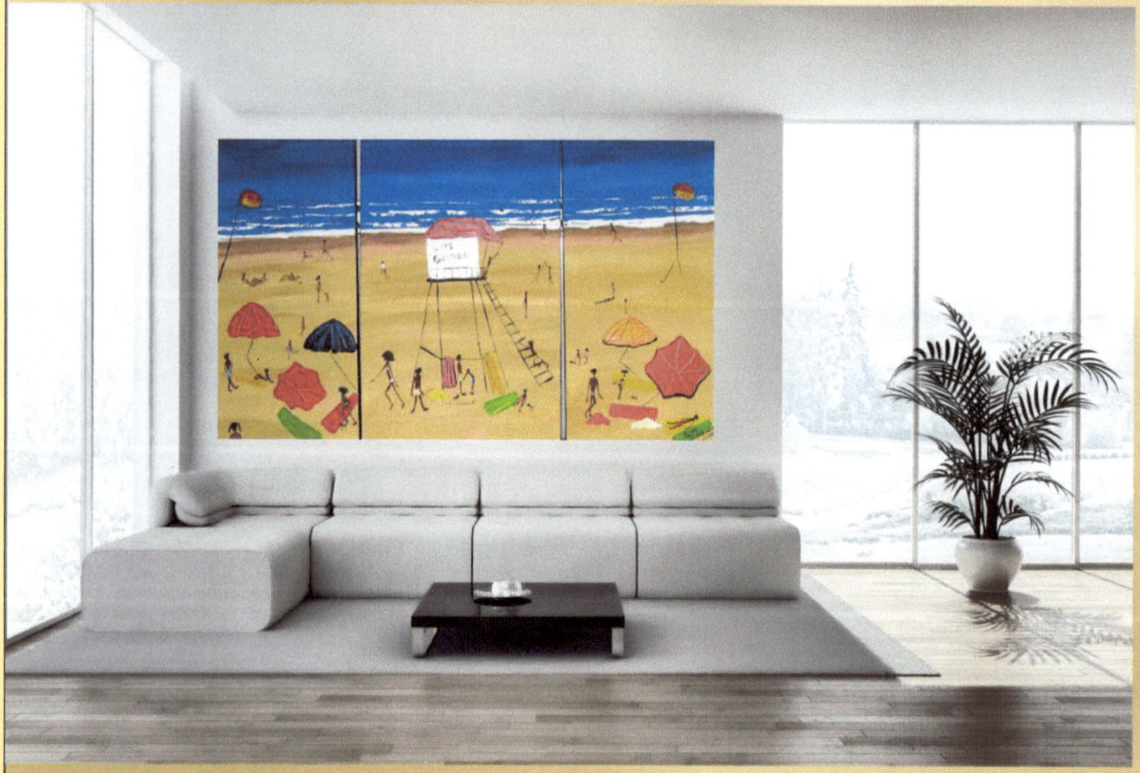

www.ingramcontent.com/pod-product-compliance
Lightning Source LLC
Chambersburg PA
CBHW050409180526
45159CB00005B/2201
* 9 7 8 1 5 1 6 9 5 2 1 8 2 *